Executive Compensation

Executive

Graef S. Crystal

Compensation

*Money,
Motivation,
and
Imagination*

Revised Edition of "Financial Motivation for Executives"

A Division of American Management Associations

Library of Congress Cataloging in Publication Data

Crystal, Graef S.
　Executive compensation.

　Edition of 1970 published under title: Financial motivation for executive.
　Includes index.
　1. Executives—Salaries, pensions, etc.—United States.　I. Title.
HD4965.5.U6C76　　　1978　　658.4'07'222　　78–17699
ISBN 0–8144–5469–0

Portions of this book were originally published under the title *Financial Motivation for Managers,* © 1970 American Management Associations.

© 1978 AMACOM
A division of American Management Associations, New York.
All rights reserved. Printed in the United States of America.

Second Printing

To Walt Carrell

The best of my many mentors

Preface

With each passing year we witness the publication of several more books on the subject of executive compensation. Some of them are limited to problems of taxation, others are concerned with the proper preparation of the necessary legal documents. Still others address the consumer of executive compensation products: the executive himself. These books give the executive pointers on how to get more out of his company and then remit less of it to Washington.

This book is different. It is directed to senior corporate managers who must decide what forms of compensation to employ and—more important—must defend their decisions in front of increasingly questioning boards of directors. It is also directed to compensation professionals, who must help senior corporate managers in their decision making and who must finally implement the approved plans.

Although this book covers the tax and accounting aspects of executive compensation—and perhaps the executive reader might even get from it a few tips that will help him personally—these are not its primary purposes. The real subject of this book is motivation. I do not believe that the pursuit of money turns everyone's head. Many people in this society are motivated very little by money, if at all. Some have entered the ministry, some have joined the Peace Corps, others work for the government or in academia.

But those who have chosen to climb the ladder in the business world are more interested in money than those who have not. They not only want to earn more; in general, they are amenable to changing their behavior to do so. For them, properly designed monetary incentives *do* work, notwithstanding the disclaimers of some psychologists. These executives and managers will sometimes work *harder* for more money, but they will almost always work *smarter* for it.

This book is designed to help those who must motivate the executives who in turn are to accomplish the goals that are important to a company's shareholders.

The point of departure for this book was my earlier one, *Finan-*

cial Motivation for Executives, published by AMA in 1970. Some parts of the earlier book—notably the first, second, and fourth chapters—have been incorporated here with minimal or minor changes.

By far the greater portion of this book, however, is, appropriately, new. Much has happened in the area of executive compensation during the past eight years. Two major tax laws have been passed by Congress, the rules governing accounting for many forms of compensation have been rewritten, and the Securities and Exchange Commission has become increasingly active. As usual, the Internal Revenue Service is always active.

Then, too, company practices have changed. Bonus plans have become much more formalized, and rules regarding bonus eligibility have been rethought. Stock options—once the sine qua non of executive compensation devices—have gone through numerous permutations within some companies and have been rejected entirely by others. In their place have arisen a welter of new and usually imaginative long-term incentive compensation devices.

All these changes are reflected in the pages of this new book.

There are two groups of people who should be acknowledged as having been of material help in the preparation of this manuscript. My clients constitute the first group. Over the years, they have taught me a great deal, most of it useful and positive. In turn, I hope I have been of help to them. The second group are the people at AMA who encouraged this project and spent considerable time seeing it through. In particular, I would like to thank my editor, Dorothy Macdonald, for her help. Ms. Macdonald edited my last book eight years ago. I assumed my prowess as a writer had been increasing at an exponential rate, but she showed me that, whatever the rate of increase, I was still in need of plenty of help. The fact that I received it, though only grudgingly gratifying to me, should be marvelously gratifying to the reader.

Graef S. Crystal

Contents

A Philosophy of Executive Compensation

America has become so successful economically that this book must perforce open on a defensive note. One price we have to pay for our affluence is the emergence of a host of individuals who claim that money no longer motivates. As critics of affluence, they have themselves become quite affluent. And so we have seemingly come full circle.

The Doctrine of Economic Man

Before discussing this "modern" development, let us go back in time. It was not too many years ago when all but a handful of the world's population lived at or below the subsistence level. These people were spared excruciating decisions as to whether this year's disposable income should be spent on a trip to Paris or on a new car. They had no disposable income. If they were able to avoid hunger on most days and provide shelter and clothing for themselves and their families, they counted themselves lucky.

As society made small advances, it became possible for a few citizens to give up "productive" work and devote themselves to studying the condition of their fellow men. Some of these individuals called themselves economists. They observed that when a man was not entirely certain that he would have enough to eat, he would tend to work as long and as hard as he could to obtain enough money to alleviate, if not remove, this uncertainty. Within the limits imposed by human physiology, this man would even double his hours of work to earn just a small amount of additional money. The fact that these additional hours were being recompensed at half time rather than time and a half or double time was immaterial because some additional money was always better than none no matter how hard one had to work to obtain it. Thus was born the doctrine of economic man.

Economic man, like the machines he was patterned after, was rational and seemingly devoid of emotions. It was always a certainty that he would take the steps necessary to maximize his income regardless of the effort it required. With economic man enshrined, the economists had an easy time of predicting future economic trends.

Time passed, productivity increased, and eventually most people in this country began to rise above the subsistence level. This evolutionary development was of little consequence for the doctrine of economic man, however, for these people had a large backlog of unsatisfied although not survival-related needs. Thus people were still interested in maximizing their incomes so they could buy a little more meat, own a second pair of shoes, and possess a roof that leaked only rarely.

The Affluent Society

More time passed. In the 1950s most people in this country had incomes which allowed them to live considerably above the subsistence level. They had meat every day, four and five pairs of shoes, and a roof that was watertight. In fact it became difficult for many people to decide how to spend their extra money.

The advertising industry rose to this new challenge. If people had no instinctual craving for an electric toothbrush or an automatic garage-door opener, they would have to be reeducated. Thus a new type of advertising industry was born whose purpose was to synthesize nonexistent needs. This led to John Kenneth Galbraith's "affluent society."

To the great distress of many economists, the doctrine of economic man showed some very distinct signs of morbidity in the new affluent society. No longer would most individuals accept a marginally lower rate of compensation just to earn a few extra dollars. Even with overtime pay at double time and triple time, it became more and more difficult to get a lot of "takers." (In periods of high inflation, as in the mid-1970s, economic man showed signs of reviving, but this was probably temporary.)

Enter the Psychologists

Into this confused state of events rode the psychologists. Being free of any formal training in economics, finance, or general business, they were able to take a fresh point of view. They proceeded to study groups of white collar workers and professional employees to see what motivated them.

The psychologists developed a gimmick—that *money no longer motivates*. This was such a revolutionary statement that it really drew the crowds. Groups of executives, who on the surface appeared to be highly money-motivated, turned out to hear the "new wisdom." The speaking schedules of these psychologists became so busy that, in order to establish some semblance of priorities, many of them responded to requests for lectures by asking, "How much are you planning to pay?" Being academics, these psychologists saw themselves as exceptions to their own rule regarding motivation.

Even some of the more avant garde economists jumped on the bandwagon. John Kenneth Galbraith in *The New Industrial State** remarked that he had yet to meet a corporate chief executive who would admit to working harder for more money. Apparently the executive was already working as hard as he could. (An unanswered question, however, is whether executives would work just as hard for more money—at a competitor firm that was willing to pay it.)

Perhaps the psychologists are right. But if they are, it is for the wrong reasons. If money no longer motivates, it is because of the inept way in which some companies handle their compensation programs. It is quite possible that the psychologists' studies were conducted at such companies.

In addition, the arguments of the "money is dead" school of psychology contain certain inconsistencies, which are discussed later. First, however, let us examine two other contemporary aspects relevant to the current value of compensation.

The Supply–Demand Crunch

We are today—and for the foreseeable future—in a seller's market for executive talent. As American business continues to grow, so does

*Boston, Mass.: Houghton Mifflin Co., 1968.

the number of executive positions. On the supply side of the equation, however, we find not an increase but a decrease owing to the low birthrate of the depression years. The "depression babies" are now in their 40s, and it is from this age group that most upper-middle management and top management positions are filled. Thus we have the classic supply-demand crunch. The result has been inevitable: a rapid increase in the compensation levels of many executive positions.

Now academics are always criticizing American business for adopting purely pragmatic approaches to problem solving. Paying more money to obtain executive talent may be inelegant, and it may also be incorrect, but to the chagrin of those who claim that money no longer motivates, it works.

In another area, however, American business is heeding the advice of the academic community. For years, the management philosophers have been preaching that a good manager can manage anything. As Don Mitchell put it in *Top Man: Reflections of a Chief Executive*, "[The good manager] can manage a bank, he can manage a railroad, and to the extent that anyone can, he can even manage the government."*

For years, too, the business community has rejected this advice on purely pragmatic grounds. If a steel manufacturer needed additional managers, why look for them in a bank? Obviously, one should get additional managers from other steel companies. This practice of industrial inbreeding naturally led to the payment of considerably varying compensation levels from industry to industry. As the supply-demand crunch hit certain industries, however, the going rate for new managers began to skyrocket and many executives became understandably concerned at the damage that these rates were doing to their precariously balanced internal equity. Faced with choosing the lesser of two evils, they therefore turned to managers in other industries—especially industries with lower compensation levels.

At about the same time, the conglomerate movement hit the United States and certain executives, who had previously been considered sound thinkers, began to assert their belief that the ability to manage assets was far more important than specific operating experience in a given industry. Thus the trend of hiring managers from other industries was given added momentum. (Banking, then characterized by low pay and a heavy stress on asset management, became an especially attractive hunting ground for executive talent.)

*AMA, 1970.

Executive transplants, like organ transplants, went through a critical period. They had to face the autoimmune reaction in their new company: a tendency to reject foreign tissue. These transplants were not given the benefit of modern immunosuppressive drugs, so only the most hardy made it, came to be accepted by their host organization, and proved the theory that a good manager can manage almost anything. Thus an increasing number of executives are adopting, on pragmatic grounds, an approach which they previously had rejected on the very same pragmatic grounds. The result has been and will continue to be the attenuation of interindustry compensation differences.

Also at work today is a trend toward the attenuation of regional compensation differences. It is more common today for an executive to move from San Francisco to New York than it was 50 years ago for him to move from Newark to New York.

Still another trend has been the gradual elimination of any stigma resulting from job changes. The term "job hopper" seems to be leaving the language because it would have to be used on too many nice people nowadays.

Enter the Executive Recruiter

The fact is that changing jobs today is a painless process. It wasn't so long ago that a manager had to undergo a good deal of anguish and expend considerable energy in changing jobs. First, he had to prepare a résumé and hope his secretary wouldn't tell anyone. Then he had to peruse the classified sections of numerous periodicals, which contained mostly "blind ads." After sending out about 50 résumés and running the risk of sending one to his own company, he began an arduous round of interviews, which required his absence from work with a frequency that could attract attention. Finally, he *might* find a better job and switch companies.

People have a natural resistance to change, and obviously an individual had to be extremely dissatisfied with his current circumstances before he would overcome his instinctive inertia. Perhaps his original dissatisfaction did not even stem from his compensation level, especially since he had very little hard information on the compensation practices of other companies.

Today we have man's answer to the bee: the executive recruiter. Like the bee, he is busy and he pollinates. Now the executive has very little inertia to overcome in changing jobs. He doesn't even have to know he is unhappy! He merely sits by his telephone and lets the recruiter come to him. Thus the slogans "no fuss, no bother" and "one-stop shopping" have found a home in the employment field.

By providing competitors' compensation information ("they're willing to pay up to $75,000 base salary plus a healthy bonus and options"), the executive recruiter gives the executive the feedback he needs in order to evaluate the adequacy of his current compensation package. The executive who is euphoric concerning his compensation before the phone rings may be somewhat less euphoric after he learns that he can make 25 percent more at a competitor.

Thus the supply-demand crunch and the executive recruiter have combined to keep compensation alive and well as a motivator of human behavior in American business. Let us turn now to a discussion of basic principles which underlie a sound, motivational executive compensation program.

The Role of Taxes

Tax rates are probably not the most important element in compensation planning, but they are worth discussing first because so many people seem obsessed by them.

There is no question that the tax rates applicable to various compensation devices are of more than passing importance. Obviously, if two devices can satisfy a set of motivational objectives and one can increase the individual's after-tax yield, that device should be adopted. But the big question is whether the alternative devices are in fact equally capable of satisfying a given set of objectives. Too many companies look first for any compensation device that promises a tax break; having found it, they clothe the plan with lofty purposes by way of rationalizing its use. Thus stock options are said to be highly motivational for a variety of reasons. As is demonstrated later, many of these reasons hold little water.

The one seemingly compelling and irrefutable reason for adopting a stock option plan was to decrease the executive's tax rate. At least that was the case in the early 1950s when stock options came into vogue. But two rounds of tax legislation—the Revenue Act of 1964 and the Tax Reform Act of 1969—battered the tax status of stock options with brutal force. And a third round—the Tax Reform Act of 1976—administered the coup de grâce. Now there is no longer any tax advantage to the stock option, and many companies have been left with a compensation device that has serious motivational deficiencies and is taxed at the same rate as other devices that have far more motivational value.

For years, conservatives around the world have been decrying the high tax rates imposed on the wealthy, claiming that these rates would undermine executive motivation—and hence the economy itself. Yet, as long as the tax rates don't become truly confiscatory, executives seem to work just as hard. Is this an argument that money no longer motivates? On the surface, the answer could be yes, but as Galbraith points out in *The Affluent Society,* most executives place primary emphasis on their pretax compensation and not their after-tax yield. To them, their pretax compensation represents a form of recognition. (More is said of this later.)

The point here, therefore, is that companies should design compensation programs primarily to motivate executives to perform better. Then and only then should the companies turn to the question of taxes—an important albeit secondary issue.

In the final analysis, tax advantages and gimmicks are ephemeral, so this factor makes it all the more important to build a compensation package on the bedrock of real motivation rather than the shifting sands of taxation.

Loyalty Versus Symbiosis

In the past, great stress has been placed on loyalty—loyalty to country, family, and company. Employees were told that their company loyalty would in time reap them great gains. It is particularly regrettable that loyalty has come to be so hollow a concept that many companies would do well to discard it altogether—or at least to play it down.

A more tenable approach to attracting, retaining, and motivating executive talent is *symbiosis,* originally a biological term the dictionary defines as a "union of two [animals or plants] which is not disadvantageous to either, or is advantageous to both." The term and the concept can be aptly applied to executive motivation. No longer is the talented executive in a totally subordinate and dependent position vis-à-vis his current employer, what with the supply-demand crunch and the emergence of the executive recruiter.

The bargaining power of the individual executive is approaching equality with his employer. Thus loyalty is out and symbiosis is in. Neither party can live without the other (and in some cases, neither can live *with* the other). Because of this, compensation plans should now be designed to encourage interdependence between the employer and the employee.

It is desirable in designing such compensation programs to assume that the individual executive is interested primarily in his own welfare and only secondarily, if at all, in the company's welfare. This is perhaps an overly harsh assumption, but once the company recognizes this fact it is less likely to get in trouble later on. The task, therefore, is to devise plans that would allow the individual executive to pursue his own self-interests both freely and unabashedly. And if in the process—accidentally, if you will—he assists the company in accomplishing its own objectives, then so much the better.

Risk Versus Reward

It is axiomatic in the investment world that reward must be commensurate with risk or no one will be interested in the particular security being offered. So, too, in the world of executive compensation must the reward equal the risk. That occupying a high executive position entails risk may not be a believable proposition to the academic community, but it is only too believable to the executive.

In Old Testament days, it was accepted practice each year for the high priest to transfer symbolically the sins of the people onto a goat and send him into the wilderness. Times really haven't changed all that much: Executives are our modern-day goats. If an executive is going to be penalized when things go wrong, whether he is at fault or not, then he must receive appropriate rewards when things go right. If executives don't receive recognition for their successes, the labor pool will largely be confirmed masochists.

Unfortunately, many companies are only too happy to affix blame but are seemingly loath to grant handsome rewards for excellent performance. Executives who receive little in the way of reward usually try to minimize their risks. Opportunities are thus lost and eventually the company stagnates—even founders.

At the executive level, a potential 10 percent merit increase is hardly a suitable reward for the risk being taken. Nor is a so-called incentive compensation plan that pays awards of 10 to 15 percent of base salary. If a company wants to attract gutsy executives who are willing to take chances, then that company must offer significant compensation when their decisions prove to be profitable. Saul Gellerman, in *Management by Motivation,** correctly surmised that a large amount of money is needed today in order to "turn on" an executive with financial incentives.

The Role of Incentives

One of the best compensation systems is used in the sports and entertainment worlds. Pay is immediately and directly related to the contributions being made—at the time they are being made.

Universally adopting the sports and entertainment world compensation patterns, however, would create sheer chaos elsewhere in society. Most of us assume not only that our talents will fail to decline, but that they will indeed continue to increase indefinitely. As a result, we are unlikely to save during our great years to tide us over our poor years. Unhappily, there are far too many actors in "theatrical homes" because of their inability to plan ahead.

Society—and business also—demands that compensation have a modicum of stability. Thus we have the base salary. It is noteworthy that the word "base" can mean "the bottom of something, considered as its foundation" and "of little value." Judging from the way in which base salaries are handled by most companies, both definitions seem particularly apt.

It is well known that base salaries go up, but they rarely go down. And because they don't decrease, most prudent managers see to it that they don't increase too quickly either. Thus base salaries tend to be inert.

To counteract the base-salary problems, years ago a number of companies devised what is known as the executive incentive compensation plan. (By attaching the word "incentive," the companies implicitly recognized that other plans, such as base salary and fringe benefits, contained little incentive.) By making these incentive payments go down as well as up, these companies were in a position to make total cash compensation (base salary plus the incentive) go down as well as up.

In adopting this approach, these companies were implicitly following accepted psychological stimulus-and-response principles first enunciated by Pavlov and then amplified by behaviorists.

Those who have raised children know that a spanking administered six months after an act of misconduct is likely to achieve noth-

*AMA, 1968.

ing. Hitting the child with a baseball bat immediately after the mis-
deed will undoubtedly eliminate any recurrence of the act, but may
eliminate the child as well. Similarly, a piece of candy given six
months after a desirable act is likely to achieve nothing. A $100 bill
given immediately after the act will probably be motivating but represents a case of overkill. The best way of handling a child is to give the
proper amount of praise or punishment at the proper time, either to
reinforce the things the child has done that are desirable or to eliminate the things that are undesirable. There has been no concrete
evidence as yet that such an approach will not work equally well on
executives.

Determining the Incentive Plan's Objectives

The key to such an approach is to determine what is desirable and
what is not. In other words, just what is it that the company wishes to
"incent"? In the business world, this question is answered all too easily
by some executives: "Obviously we want profits." These executives
unfortunately have failed to realize that although most incentive
plans do motivate behavioral changes, the end result may be different
from what they had anticipated. Two case histories illustrate:

> In an article in a reputable business magazine, a former plant
> general manager of an electronics firm is described as having
> given ". . . wide authority to decide which products [the plant
> managers] would make. Since each manager was evaluated on the
> basis of the profitability of his plant, the managers chose the
> products that were easiest to make—those already in production
> with high yields. Only reluctantly would the managers start new
> products."
> In a similar magazine, another article reported that a large
> conglomerate was having profit troubles in one of its major divi-
> sions. It was stated that "One reason, ironically, may have been an
> overemphasis on immediate profits. By tying managers' incen-
> tives to their current return on gross assets, the firm may have
> inadvertently discouraged them from spending enough on re-
> search and development."

Can the managers of these companies be blamed for their performance? Did the incentive plans at these companies fail? Surely the
answer to both questions is a resounding no. The plans stressed current profits, and therefore the executives were motivated to maximize
current profits. There was nothing in the plans about spending suffi-

cient funds on research and development or on taking other steps to ensure that the company was profitable *over the long term.*

In discussing these incentive plan pitfalls with certain executives, one may be chided for failing to take executive judgment into account. "My men aren't going to louse up the company's future by cutting their R&D expenditures just to get a few bucks more bonus. They're going to do what's *right.*" Yet sitting back and hoping that one's executives will do what's right is no way to run a company. Moreover, an incentive plan which requires executives to override the incentive aspects of the plan in order to do what's right can only be termed idiotic. A properly designed incentive plan should be a stepping-stone to accomplishment, not a hurdle placed in the executive's path.

The fact is that people see incentive plans through their own self-interested eyes, and therefore the company should be absolutely sure that it is encouraging its executives to do exactly what it wants done before initiating the plan.

In an effort to increase the number of its Christmas Club accounts, one bank devised a seemingly simple and appealing incentive plan. Each teller was to receive 1,000 trading stamps for each new account of $25 or more. Since most of the tellers were women, the idea of using trading stamps, rather than cash, was a masterstroke. (This plan was implemented in the days when Betty Friedan's name was a household word only in the Friedan household.) The plan worked, but not the way its designers anticipated. On the very first day, an officer overheard the following conversation between a customer and a teller.

Customer: I'd like to open a $500 Christmas Club account.

Teller (batting her eyelids): Sir, we're having a contest for Christmas Club accounts and I get 1,000 trading stamps for each account of $25 or more that I open. Would you mind terribly if I opened 20 new accounts for you?

Well, back to the drawing board!

Looking to the Long Term

Psychological research has shown that it takes less reward to motivate individuals toward accomplishing short-range goals than long-range goals. This is particularly true of Americans, for we are known around the world as a very impatient people. Most companies' incentive plans, unfortunately, are oriented toward the accomplishment of such short-range goals as current profits, as illustrated by the cases just mentioned. Yet increasingly complex technology forces us to take a longer and longer time to develop new products. These products require tremendous capital investments, often with no return for many years. Consider the case of the Boeing Co. In 1955, it decided to develop and produce a plane subsequently known as the 707. It was not until 1959, however, that the first plane was delivered to the airlines and not until 1965, some ten years after the original decision to produce the plane, that Boeing recorded its first dollar of profit on this fabulously successful aircraft. (It is worthy of note that when Boeing won the multibillion-dollar supersonic transport (SST) contract, its stock dropped rather than rose. Investors correctly surmised that the project could only hurt Boeing's earnings over the short term.)

Most companies fall into the trap of basing their incentive plans on annual results simply because they must make annual reports to their shareholders. A plan based on annual results is valid only if the results and the decisions related to them were made in the same year. In many companies, continually longer product lead times have caused the decisions to be made in one year and the results to occur in another. A more viable approach, therefore, is to center an incentive plan around the company's typical product development cycle. Thus the plan might be oriented to achieving results two years, three years, or five years hence. That is not to say that rewards would not be paid during the intervening period, however, since the executives could receive either "progress payments" on future goals or payments for results stemming from past product development cycles.

Tying incentive systems to the accomplishment of longer-range corporate objectives has a significant side effect: The objectives themselves are likely to be established more accurately. The five-year plans of a number of companies are currently nothing more than exercises in extrapolation. For example, sales in 1976 were 20 percent higher than in 1975. Therefore, a 20 percent escalation factor has been used for each of the following five years. So it is with manufacturing costs, selling expenses, and profits. Such a plan looks good and gives the company an aura of progressiveness, but it accomplishes nothing. Indeed, it may obscure vital developments that, unless properly handled, will lead to trouble.

When management incentives are tied to future plans, however, there is less likelihood of a simple extrapolation because it could result in a significant loss of incentive compensation if it turns out to represent a spurious estimate of the company's future performance.

Keeping Rewards Meaningful

Once the objectives are properly established, the designer of a viable incentive system must provide significant rewards for the attainment of these objectives. As mentioned earlier, a payment of 10 to 15 percent of salary is unlikely to motivate most executives to take any significant business risks. Regrettably, few companies are willing to grant the significant rewards required. This results in the loss of valuable executive talent.

Take the case of H. Ross Perot, founder of Electronic Data Systems Corp. According to a November 1968 *Fortune* article, Mr. Perot first encountered the unwillingness of certain employers to pay for performance when he was still a boy. He had established a newspaper route ". . . in an area that the newspaper hadn't considered worth cultivating. Perot traveled 20 miles a day on horseback to deliver the papers, and because he had started the route, he received 70 percent of the price instead of the customary 30 percent. When the route began to thrive, the newspaper tried to reverse the ratio." The article goes on to indicate that Perot was successful in arguing the newspaper out of its plan. Later in his life, he was not so successful:

> The origins of this incredible bonanza [his founding of Electronic Data Systems] go back to the day in early 1962 when International Business Machines Corporation decided that Perot, one of its Dallas salesmen, was earning too much money. As Perot recalls it, IBM wanted to spread its commissions as evenly as possible among the salesmen, preferring not to let any individual make an inordinate amount. In 1962, Perot, who had joined the company in 1957, sold his year's quota of computers by mid-January. He then was kept in the office, where he found little to do but think subversive thoughts about his employer.

Mr. Perot subsequently put his subversive thoughts into action, much to IBM's detriment.

Some companies rationalize their failure to pay meaningful incentive awards by citing the specter of adverse stockholder reaction. One company president was visibly upset when 6 percent of his company's stockholders voted *against* a new incentive plan. Yet, not too long after, another company submitted a proposal to its stockholders to *reduce* the size of its incentive compensation funds and received the same 6 percent adverse stockholder vote!

Now, this is not to imply that one should overlook the interests of the stockholders and expect that they will approve any plan management cares to present. Stockholders are part of a symbiotic equation; they are looking out for their own self-interests, but at the same time they are dependent on company management. Therefore, they are likely to be attracted to only those plans that promise them a high percentage of the company's additional earnings. Except for the professional dissidents, few stockholders are likely to begrudge a company $5 million in bonus funds, if the funds are paid only when they receive $25 million in additional earnings.

Viewed in this light, incentive plans cost little or nothing when they lead to the attainment of the goals for which they were designed.

The Recognition Principle

Let us turn once again to those psychologists who say that money no longer motivates. They affirmed that motivation is a multifaceted thing. They discovered that some factors motivate primarily in a positive direction. An increase in these factors leads to greater motivation, but a decrease leads to little "demotivation." They also discovered that some other factors motivate in a negative direction. An increase in these factors does *not* lead to greater motivation but a decrease causes a good deal of *de*motivation. Working conditions, fringe benefits, and money belong in the second category. Such factors as the challenge of the job itself and recognition are considered motivators.

Few forms of recognition available to a company are as tangible as money. It follows that if recognition motivates and money can be used as a form of recognition, money can motivate.

Recognition is a relative phenomenon, however. Some individuals must receive a lot more than others for them to feel that they have received proper recognition. Cruel though it sounds, there can be no winner unless there are losers. It is questionable whether Olympic milers would run as hard as they do if everyone who crossed the finish line received the same gold medal and the same salute from the crowd.

A number of Communist countries are painfully aware that failure to use the recognition principle in compensation creates adverse results. Analyzing the low productivity of the Communist countries of

Eastern Europe, *Time* magazine stated that "Under Socialism there is . . . almost no difference in pay between the worker who sweats over his machine and the non-worker who would rather flirt with shop girls, chat with colleagues, or take innumerable breaks. . . ." *Time* went on to report that a favorite expression among Communist workers is, "Whether you sit or stand, you make two grand."

It is regrettable that the compensation practices of too many companies in the United States bear an uncomfortable resemblance to those of Eastern Europe. At these companies everyone "gets a little something." And because everyone gets a little something, there are rarely enough funds left over to give the outstanding performers outstanding rewards. Of course, the outstanding executives may make 8 or 10 percent more than their mediocre counterparts, but they should be making 50 and 60 percent more if there is to be real recognition. The result is that the outstanding performers leave for greener pastures and the mediocre performers stay on. (Where else could they get such a good deal?) And it is the company that is ultimately the big loser.

Companies that are able to maintain significant compensation differentials between outstanding and mediocre performers seem to have less trouble in keeping executive talent over the short term— even when their overall compensation posture is below average—than companies whose compensation practices are above average but who consistently fail to provide the proper degree of performance recognition. This situation exists because individual employees, like the companies for which they work, are constantly surveying their "competitors" to assess the adequacy of their compensation. In this case, an employee's competitors are not in other companies, however, but are within his own firm. Hence, most employees make a point of finding out what their peers are being paid. Since they also have some well-defined opinions as to their peers' performance, they are in a position to determine, albeit subjectively, whether their own compensation is equitable. If an executive finds inequities, he becomes particularly susceptible to the blandishments of the executive recruiter when he calls to bring news of the compensation marketplace.

The Need for Guts

Most executives share two reactions in common when they are considering compensation increases (including bonuses) for their subordinates. First, most executives share the universal desire to be loved by everyone—or, to state the reverse, not to be hated. This pressure from below makes it exceedingly difficult for an executive to withhold an increase from his subordinate. Thus we have the so-called token increase, an award of generally 4 to 5 percent of salary or less. (There have been merit increases as low as $100 per year for a $25,000 executive.)

Second, virtually every executive assiduously cultivates an image of cost-consciousness. To be labeled a spendthrift is akin to damnation. This pressure from above makes it exceedingly difficult for the executive to give his subordinate much more than a 10 percent increase—and very often, his natural timorousness is reinforced by a formal company policy limiting compensation increases.

When confronted with pressure from above and below, many executives scuttle behind the average for safety. Thus, in many companies, if the average compensation increase is 7 percent of salary, better than 90 percent of all increases just happen to fall between 6 and 8 percent. The average, whatever other pitfalls it may possess, is always psychologically safe. Who, after all, can be criticized for granting an average increase?

Man's capacity to rationalize seems to be infinite, and virtually any rationalization that comes to mind will do when it comes to justifying a compensation increase for an individual who should have none. Thus events outside the individual's control are used to explain why a small bonus is being given to someone who deserves no bonus at all. (How many times have you seen someone voluntarily relinquish a large bonus when events outside his control were the cause of his great success?) Or the fear is expressed that withholding a bonus, where one has been paid in previous years, will seriously compromise the individual's standard of living, notwithstanding the fact that he has been warned repeatedly not to count on the bonus.

Thus we have a leveling process in compensation. Where the range of merit increases should be between zero and 20 percent of salary, it is more likely between 6 and 10 percent. Where the range of bonuses should be between 15 and 75 percent of salary, it is more likely between 20 and 25 percent. The funds used to pay increases or bonuses to those who should have none necessarily come out of the pockets of those whose performance is outstanding, but unrecognized. After all, no company has an unlimited amount of compensation dollars to spend. Small wonder that the psychologists say money doesn't motivate!

Compensation leveling becomes more widespread during inflationary periods. A few years ago, the cost of living was rising at about

10 percent annually, and many managers were given salary increase funds of only 10 or 11 percent of payroll to distribute. These managers realized that to give an employee an increase of less than 10 percent was tantamount to cutting his pay in real terms, and they couldn't bring themselves to take such an action. On the other hand, they also realized that the outstanding employee rightfully ought to receive a real increase in pay, over and above the cost-of-living increase, of perhaps 7 to 10 percent. However, being well aware of the top management precept that a 10 percent increase bordered on the exorbitant, they were reluctant to risk their own careers to get a 20 percent increase for a deserving subordinate. Besides, they had already given the relatively poorest performers a 10 percent increase to keep them even with the cost of living, and there was no extra money. So we can add one more victim to those most hurt by inflation: the outstanding performer.

As stated previously, the motivational value of compensation lies primarily in the recognition it bestows on the recipient. To achieve the spread of compensation actions that is necessary to afford the proper degree of recognition requires guts. It takes guts to withhold an increase or a bonus from someone who is undeserving. It takes guts to fight the system and get superlative rewards for a truly outstanding performer. Above all, it takes guts to recognize the handy rationalizations for what they are and to stay away from the psychological safety of the average.

Yet few of us seem to possess the kind of guts required. Take tipping, for example. In principle, we all endorse the belief that a bad waiter should get no tip and an excellent waiter should get a better-than-average tip—say 20 to 25 percent of the bill. But how many of us have the guts to "stare down" a hostile waiter confronted with an empty change plate? One way or another, most of us rationalize and pay him his 15 percent, promising ourselves that "the next time will be different." On the other hand, we are loath to pay the superlative waiter much more than 15 percent, because after all we have already spent plenty on the incompetents. Is it any wonder that excellent waiters are a rarity and that the restaurant industry suffers from a plethora of mediocrity?

Minimizing Turnover

The compensation objectives of virtually every company include the minimization of employee turnover. For all our sophistication in other areas, however, we still conceive of turnover as quantitative and not possessing qualitative aspects. The true turnover goal is not to reduce the absolute number of resignations but to reduce the number of resignations from outstanding personnel, while simultaneously increasing those from mediocre personnel. Compensation systems, if properly designed, can aid in attaining this important objective.

An effort should be made to see that one's outstanding personnel receive outstanding compensation compared not only with what lesser performers get within the organization, but especially with what one's competitors pay to their outstanding performers. Such an approach makes it highly difficult for a competitor to steal a superb performer, unless he is offering a significant promotional opportunity (and, from a compensation standpoint, there is no effective way to guard against this eventuality; like the Marines, a company should plan on taking at least some losses).

An effort should also be made to see that one's mediocre personnel are paid less than the minimum rates of one's competitors. (Of course, it is the rare company which admits to having failed to weed out all mediocrity, but statistically there have to be as many mediocre personnel in the United States as outstanding ones, and they must be somewhere!) If these people subsequently quit, partly owing to their low salaries, the company gains from it because by again "drawing from the deck," it has a better-than-even chance of "improving its hand." And if these people quit to join a competitor, then the company gains a double advantage. Filling a Trojan horse with one's incompetent personnel and shipping it to a competitor is a promising and too-little-used business tactic.

Avoiding the Golden Handcuffs Approach

The stages of maturation of a typical company are very similar to the stages of human maturation. First, the new company has an entrepreneurial flavor, and its compensation program consists of very low base salaries and very high-risk compensation devices, such as stock options. As the company approaches adulthood, its compensation blend tends to approach the normal. The stability increases and the risks decrease. As the company becomes middle-aged, it tends, like middle-aged people, to concern itself with consolidating its gains and minimizing its risks.

It is at this point that many companies hit upon forcible income deferrals as the answer to their problems. These deferrals most commonly occur in the company's incentive compensation program, and the most common approach is to require that each bonus be paid not immediately but in a series of annual installments, starting either with the year of the award or after retirement. The rub is that any deferred amounts which have not yet been paid are forfeited if the individual voluntarily resigns. Thus these compensation devices have come to be known as the golden handcuffs approach.

Companies employing this approach euphemistically describe it as an incentive for the individual to remain with the company. From their standpoint this may well be true, but in the eyes of the individual it is a disincentive to leave and as such is almost uniformly resented.

There is some evidence that the golden handcuffs approach actually does keep some people from leaving, but, by and large, the only thing that is consistently maintained is the level of employee mediocrity. Those whose performance is outstanding are easily "bought out" by a competitor. And since this motivational device is at best negatively oriented, an offer of employment involving a more positively cast motivational approach is all the more readily welcomed.

The fact that the individual's actual compensation is less than his nominal compensation during his all-important early years as an executive is still another reason why the golden handcuffs approach, far from keeping outstanding personnel, makes them increasingly receptive to the offers of the competition. To illustrate, assume that an executive with a $40,000 base salary receives a $20,000 bonus, payable in five equal annual installments. The executive's nominal total cash compensation is $60,000, but during the first year of such an arrangement, his actual cash flow compensation is $44,000, consisting of his $40,000 base salary and the first installment of his bonus. It is not until five years have passed and four more $20,000 bonuses have been granted that the executive is receiving the $60,000 the company says he is receiving. Meanwhile, the executive is highly susceptible to a competitor's offer of the same $60,000 total cash compensation if it is to be paid to him all at once.

Obviously, the problems with the golden handcuffs approach also work in reverse. A company that pays its bonuses in installments is undoubtedly going to have a tough time attracting an executive from a company that pays its bonuses in a lump sum.

Psychic Income

Not all elements in a company's compensation program can be measured in dollars. This is particularly the case with status symbols which provide a sort of psychic income to the individual and therefore must be considered within the framework of executive compensation.

Status symbols are used most frequently in such historical institutions as the army. This type of institution is generally characterized by high psychic income and low cash compensation. Although individuals obviously do not join the army solely because of its status symbols, there appears to be some willingness to trade status for cash.

Status symbols lead a rather schizophrenic life in American business. On the one hand, evidence of their use is rife, what with posh executive offices which vary in size according to the level of the position, water pitchers, banana plants, limousines, and the like. On the other hand, there is a very vocal antistatus movement in almost every company. Some executives say that status symbols are completely useless; it's the size of the little old paycheck that really counts. They generally make such statements from behind a polished mahogany desk in their multi-windowed, lushly carpeted offices.

Status symbols are alive and well in the executive suite. They fill a genuine human need, and so it is unfortunate that people who appreciate them are made uncomfortable by those who probably appreciate them even more but refuse to admit it. Status symbols are particularly important in business, because how else is one to tell the players apart? Wearing a tie used to have some distinction but it no longer does. And publicly revealing the size of one's compensation package is considered poor form in most social circles. (This is somewhat regrettable because if cash compensation is truly being used as recognition and is then shrouded in secrecy, its motivational value is diminished.)

A prime executive status symbol today is the stock option. Although the amount of compensation it produces may bear little or no relation to the executive's performance, the fact that he has the option and is a "member of the club" bears significantly on his psychic income.

Indeed, even the "underwater" stock option is not without some value. It may be poor form to brag about the size of one's salary or bonus at a neighborhood cocktail party, but it is quite acceptable to lament that one's stock option isn't worth the paper it's printed on, thereby engendering not only sympathy but respect for one's apparently lofty position in the corporate pecking order.

Far from being eliminated, therefore, status symbols should be exploited on a reasonable and well-controlled basis. Their continued use, despite constant criticism, shows their utility and durability. More important, they represent a relatively inexpensive form of compensation to the company. A $1,000 carpet placed in an executive's office (provided that not everyone has a carpet) may well be worth a good deal more than a $1,000 salary increase (although if he is asked, the executive will undoubtedly deny it), and in any event its cost, unlike the salary increase, is not borne every year.

The Need for Individualization

A growing body of research in the behavioral sciences has demonstrated that compensation is viewed somewhat subjectively and not always in direct proportion to the money involved. Two experiments, one providing direct evidence and the other indirect evidence, illustrate this finding.

1. A group of psychologists interviewed each employee of an industrial firm and asked him how much he thought the firm was contributing on his behalf to the company retirement plan. The employees, like those of most companies, had never been informed as to the amount the company was contributing, and thus they were forced to guess. The data analysis showed a distinct and not very surprising pattern: Younger employees consistently underestimated the company's contributions to the retirement plan, and older employees just as consistently overestimated them.

2. Children drawn from both high and low socioeconomic backgrounds were seated in front of a machine which could be manipulated to project a circle of light of any diameter on a screen. They were then asked to use their memory to adjust the circle of light until it approximated the size of a quarter. Almost uniformly, the children from low socioeconomic backgrounds made the quarter look like a half-dollar. Conversely, the children from high socioeconomic backgrounds made the quarter look like a dime.

Other experiments have shown that the value an individual places on various types of compensation changes over a period of time in accordance with his current needs. Thus the young executive who is raising three children hasn't the slightest interest in retirement income, but as he begins to approach retirement he is likely to change his opinion.

Because of these findings—and just plain common sense—some companies have begun to move away from an approach which dictates precisely how the individual's compensation package is to be structured and to offer him at least some degree of choice. Usually, this individualization first occurs in the company's bonus awards. The executive is permitted to choose from among various combinations of immediate cash and deferred income payments, and he can vary his choice from year to year. If he defers some income, he is often given the choice as to how such income is to be invested—say, in government bonds, company stock, or a mutual fund. He is also permitted to decide whether the dividends and interest received from the investments are to be paid to him in cash as they are produced or reinvested in the same types of securities from which they arose. Finally, the executive can decide when his deferred payments are to commence and the number of years over which the payout will occur.

Such an approach lets the younger executive with small children take his bonus entirely in cash to meet his pressing financial needs. As time passes and his income rises, the executive may decide to defer some portion of his bonus, with the payout slated to start when the children reach college age. At that time, the executive will probably revert to a total cash bonus; and by using this money plus the earlier deferrals, he can mitigate the financial burdens of sending several children through college at the same time. When his children finally become financially independent, the executive will probably elect to defer all of his bonus until his retirement. Of course, that is not always the pattern. On occasion, one finds the younger executive with substantial outside income and an accompanying desire to defer all of his bonus. One also finds the executive in his sixties who is still sending children through college and, although interested in providing more retirement income, simply can't afford it.

These exceptions wreak havoc with the "fixed choice" approach used by some companies as their answer to individualization. At these companies, all executives below, say, age 40 are paid their bonuses in cash. Those between 40 and 45 receive two-thirds of their bonus in cash and have the remaining one-third deferred. The ratio reverses between 45 and 50, and after age 50 the entire bonus is deferred. At other companies, a more elaborate matrix approach is used involving not only age but base salary and salary grade. These fixed-choice approaches offer a sort of planned individualization, but they still do not give the individual executive any real choice.

The Resistance to Individualization

If giving the executive a choice as to the form and timing of at least part of his compensation package makes such eminent sense, why has this approach not been universally adopted? One reason is usually given, but there is probably another reason also.

First, there is the argument that the administrative costs of individualization are prohibitive. With electronic data processing and a limited number of participating executives, this argument holds little water. One company which individualized its bonus plan reports that the whole process is handled by a single IBM card completed once each year and by a rather simple computer program. Of course, it will always cost something to individualize, but the benefits to be derived clearly outweigh these costs.

A less obvious but more real reason for opposing individualization is the authority that top management must of necessity relinquish to the individual executive. Some company presidents say, "Why should I give them a choice? All they will do is take everything in cash and squander it. Then they'll blame me for not providing for their retirement. No sir, I know what is best for my executives." It is somewhat ironic that these same executives who cannot be trusted to be reasonably prudent in managing their own financial affairs are assigned considerable responsibility for being prudent in the management of their company's affairs!

In today's environment of rising compensation costs and tight profit margins, executives who oppose individualization on essentially irrational grounds should reconsider their position. If one individual perceives $1 of retirement income to be worth $2 and another perceives the same $1 to be worth only 25 cents, it makes a good deal of sense to give the first individual a lot of retirement income and find some more appealing alternative for the second. In this way the company can lower its net costs of compensation and, as long as not every company is following the individualization principle, enhance its ability to attract and retain qualified executive talent.

One note of caution should be injected here, however. Some companies have adopted the individualization principle but have then tied it to the golden handcuffs approach. Thus the executive can take his bonus immediately in cash or can defer it, but if he chooses the latter, he stands to forfeit any unpaid installments in the event that he quits his job before they are received. Obviously, few executives are likely to accept this offer of deferrals. Such an approach therefore represents individualization in name only and generally causes nothing but resentment. It would be better not to individualize at all than to offer what amounts to a hollow promise.

Preparing for Obsolescence

Long ago, all companies discovered that machinery and equipment eventually wear out or become obsolete. And the greater the demands on the equipment and the faster the growth in technology, the more rapid the process. As a result, provision is made for accumulating reserves for the replacement of this machinery and equipment. Yet when it comes to executives, the same rules never seem to be applied.

There is equally abundant evidence that executives also wear out eventually. And the greater the demands on him and the faster the growth in management technology, the sooner he becomes obsolete.

Most companies tend to take one of two approaches to meet this problem. The first approach is to reassign the executive to an innocuous position with a high-sounding title. Since this fools neither the executive nor his peers, a rather handsome salary increase is usually given also. That fools no one either.

Such an approach rarely works well. The executive generally knows that his performance is inadequate, for most of us, in our heart of hearts, have a pretty realistic picture of our abilities. The executive also knows that such an approach violates good management practice and should not be adopted. He knows further that none of his peers has been deceived by his new "promotion." These conflicts often make the executive feel insecure and angry. He does himself no good; he does the company no good and may actually hurt it by spreading his "poison" to others. Moreover, younger executives who believe that the company follows sound management practice are often disillusioned by such action.

The second approach is to beef up the company qualified retirement plan and liberalize the early retirement provisions. There are valid reasons for taking this approach, and they must not be discounted. Sometimes, however, the only reason a company has for improving its retirement plan is to eliminate executive deadwood by providing an incentive to retire early.

Restructuring a company's qualifed retirement plan to handle a few cases of executive obsolescence is like using an elephant gun to kill a fly. Retirement plan benefits cannot by law favor higher-salaried personnel, but must be applied uniformly to all—or almost all—the company's employees. The costs of using the retirement plan for this purpose are therefore staggering.

Both of these approaches have one characteristic in common:

They are adopted by mediocre companies whose top management has no guts. Above all, it takes guts to face squarely a problem of executive obsolescence and remove the individual from the firm. Unfortunately, this is a cruel solution, especially when the executive has given the best years of his life in the service of his company and will probably suffer financially.

There is a more viable alternative that should be considered. Why not adopt a liberal executive severance policy which provides for salary continuation in the event of discharge (or what is known euphemistically as a management-initiated termination)? The length of salary continuation could depend on length of service with the company and could provide as much as full pay until normal retirement age for executives who are past the age of 55 and have been employed by the company for 20 years or more.

This rather simple approach will probably be met with two basic objections. First, it gives the executive something for nothing; it rewards incompetence. Yet giving the executive a fancy position with no real responsibilities or liberalizing the retirement plan to encourage early retirement can also be criticized for the very same reasons.

Liberalized severance payments will probably be criticized on grounds of cost also. Over a long term, these payments can build up to a considerable figure, and the costs could be incurred during the years when the company can least afford them. But why not establish reserves for executive obsolescence in much the same way that reserves are established for replacement of machinery and equipment? In effect, the company realistically estimates the amount of obsolescence it is likely to have and then sets aside a given amount of money each year to fund the severance plan. If such a long-term approach is taken, the costs in any one year should be minimal.

Although removing an obsolete executive may cost money, the costs will be even higher if the company retains the executive in a phoney position and allows him to make a negative contribution rather than no contribution at all. The costs of liberalizing the retirement plan are of course still higher.

Basically, the company must face the certainty—not merely the probability—that executive obsolescence will occur. The company must therefore adopt an approach that will solve the problem at the least possible cost. Facing the problem of executive obsolence is very uncomfortable, however, partly because the plan one develops may ultimately apply to oneself.

Eleven principles of sound compensation planning have been discussed in this chapter. Briefly stated, they are as follows.

1. Whenever possible, adopt plans that increase the individual's after-tax yield, but don't sacrifice motivation on the altar of taxation.
2. Establish a truly symbiotic relationship with executives rather than rely on their company loyalty.
3. Keep the reward commensurate with the risk.
4. Determine just what it is the company really wants and then "incent" it with meaningful rewards.
5. Understand the principle of recognition, and see to it that outstanding performers receive a great deal more than merely mediocre ones do.
6. Put less emphasis on minimizing total turnover and be more concerned with keeping outstanding performers and getting rid of poor ones.
7. Avoid the golden handcuffs approach. Think positively, not negatively.
8. Stress the intelligent use of status symbols and other forms of low-cost psychological gratification.
9. Provide at least some degree of individualization in the executive compensation package.
10. Face and adequately prepare for the inevitable problem of executive obsolescence.
11. Above all, have the guts to follow all these principles.

Executive
Position
Evaluation _____ 2

Essentially, there are four variables which enter into the determination of an individual's compensation.

1. *Basic responsibilities:* the major duties which the executive has been assigned.
2. *Scope of responsibilities:* the size of the organization which the executive leads or to which he provides staff services.
3. *Supply-demand:* the differential value which the marketplace assigns to varying positions over varying periods of time.
4. *Performance:* the manner in which the executive discharges the responsibilities he has been assigned.

Executive position evaluation concerns the first three variables and is the subject of this chapter.

A number of approaches to determining the value of executive positions have been tried over the years, but today only two basic approaches are used by the great majority of companies. The first is the point-factor method and the second is the marketplace method.

The Point-Factor Method of Position Evaluation

The point-factor approach involves the initial determination of those factors which seem to explain why one position is more complex and more responsible than another. In practice, the number of factors seems to be limited only by the imagination of the designer. Thus we have plans with only three factors and some with as many as fifteen or more. Although each company assigns different names to the factors it has chosen, all the plans have separate factors for education and experience.

Each factor contains a series of descriptions which cover the various possible levels, or degrees, of that factor. For example, under education the degrees might be high school graduation, A.A., A.B. or B.S., M.A. or M.S., and Ph.D.

Each degree is assigned a number of points. For example, an A.B. degree might carry 150 points; an M.A., 200 points; and a Ph.D., 300 points. The maximum number of points available on any one factor (the points assigned to the highest degree) often varies from factor to factor, thereby causing some factors to have a higher weight in the overall point score. Thus, if the points assigned to the maximum degree of each factor total 2,000 and those for the education and experience factors are 400 and 600, respectively, then education is implicitly assigned 20 percent of the total weight in the plan and experience, 30 percent.

The company's compensation personnel (sometimes a management committee) then analyze all the executive positions, using the point-factor plan. The applicable degree of each factor is chosen to match the characteristics of the position being analyzed and the points are totaled. Now we have a ranking of all the executive positions but are lacking their dollar value. That is the next step.

Certain executive positions are then chosen for survey purposes. As a group, they are called *benchmark* positions because the dollar values of the entire structure will eventually be tied to the value of these positions.

Positions are chosen as benchmarks when the company believes that positions with a similar mix of duties and responsibilities can readily be found on approximately the same organization level in competitor firms. The distribution of benchmarks is usually established so that there is a good vertical and horizontal cross-section of the company's organization: vertical through the various levels of management and horizontal through the various functional disciplines such as marketing, personnel, and engineering.

The salary rates paid by the firms surveyed are then plotted graphically against the already determined point values of the benchmark positions, and a trend line develops. This trend line permits a monetary value to be assigned to any given point value, even one which is not surveyed directly.

The last step in the point-factor evaluation process involves the grouping of point values into salary grades (for example, positions with 200 to 250 points are assigned to salary grade 4; positions with 251 to 300 points are assigned to salary grade 5) and the development of minimum and maximum amounts to be paid for each.

The point-factor evaluation plan, like all evaluation plans, has two major objectives: to insure that the company's salary structure is both internally equitable and externally competitive. Ostensibly, the point-factor plan achieves both these objectives, since executive positions are ranked internally, after which the ranks are anchored to the marketplace through a survey of competitive going rates. However, the value of point-factor plans is illusory.

In a properly designed plan, each factor should represent a discrete entity. What the entity measures should not be measured simultaneously by any other factors. Whether a point-factor plan actually consists of discrete factors can be determined by statistical factor analysis or intercorrelations. To illustrate, let us assume that 100 executive positions have been evaluated using a point-factor plan. The 100 different point values for factor A are then compared with the 100 different values for factor B. If the two factors are truly discrete, there should be no correlation (or at the very least a low correlation on the order of 0.2 to 0.3) between them. Similar correlations are also run between factor A and factor C, factor B and factor C, and every other possible combination of factors. Intercorrelations are also run between each factor and the total number of points produced.

The ideal point-factor plan produces a very low correlation between factors and between each factor and the total number of points produced. Regrettably, however, few point-factor plans even approach the ideal. Experience has shown that there is usually a considerable degree of factor contamination in every plan, such that each factor correlates very highly (around 0.9 to 0.95) with every other factor and with the total. Obviously, the factors used in these plans are not measuring discrete variables but essentially are measuring the same thing in different ways. In fact, in most plans, all but one factor can be discarded (it makes little difference which one is retained) and the points on it can be used to establish the structure. The result would not be significantly different from that produced by using the multiple factors originally designed.

One company went to a lot of trouble designing an executive

point-factor evaluation plan. Being very conscientious, the compensation personnel decided to validate the plan by comparing it with those of other companies. So masses of information were compiled on each executive position—including exhaustive position descriptions, organization charts, and work flow diagrams—and this information, which stood fully two feet high when assembled, was sent to 47 companies. Each company was asked to analyze the information on each position and evaluate the position into a hypothetical salary structure using its own method of position evaluation.

The results of this study showed that the company's executive position evaluation plan was indeed a valid instrument in that its evaluations closely matched those of the 47 companies surveyed. At least that was the conclusion reached from a superficial analysis of the data. A more detailed analysis, however, revealed that the 47 companies used 47 different methods of evaluation. Some companies had point-factor plans with three factors; some had plans with ten factors; some had no factors at all. Yet, whatever the method, all the companies came up with essentially the same result. Again, a single, global evaluation factor, not a series of discrete entities, seemed to be operating in the evaluation process. The expert in charge of compensation at that company would have done well to discard his own plan (which was rather complex) and adopt the simplest plan being used by one of the companies in the survey. Since the results weren't going to differ very much anyway, he might as well have saved himself some work!

The Effect of Supply and Demand

If point-factor plans were harmless and cost nothing but time, that wouldn't be too bad. But there is further evidence to suggest that most of these plans can cause serious damage to a company's compensation program.

No matter what names are used, the great bulk of the weight in almost all point-factor plans is placed on education and experience. And, for a given level of education and experience, the points are going to be the same, regardless of what position is being evaluated. Thus, if the personnel vice-president's position calls for a master's degree and ten years of experience and so does the financial vice-president's position, both will receive the same points for education and experience. And both are likely to end up in the same salary grade because education and experience (factors which are the hardest to evaluate accurately) account for the greatest influence on the total point score. Unfortunately, such a conclusion is in direct opposition to what the marketplace says the positions are worth. Because of supply and demand, and perhaps other variables as well, a finance executive today earns a good deal more than a personnel executive.

If the company decides to peg the salary grade of the finance and personnel executives to the market value of the latter's position, it won't be long before the employee in the former position becomes a former employee! If, on the other hand, the company decides to peg the salary grade of the finance and personnel executives to the finance executive's position, it will have needlessly increased its compensation costs. Further needless costs will probably follow because the finance executive makes it a point to keep up with current compensation trends, and he knows he should be earning a good deal more than the personnel executive. It will never occur to him that he is amply paid and the personnel executive overpaid. All he knows is that he should earn more, and if the personnel executive is paid x, he naturally should be paid $1.5x$.

A further problem with the point-factor approach to position evaluation is that it causes a mystique to be built up around the evaluation process. Of course, this is not a problem but an advantage for some individuals in the compensation field. When challenged by management in other disciplines as to why a certain position was evaluated in a certain salary grade, such individuals have been heard to reply, "You'll just have to take my word for it, because it would be impossible for a person with your background to understand the evaluation process without a great deal of study."

Such putdowns may be ego-gratifying to the individual doing the putting down, but they only hurt the compensation image of the company. Since managers in other disciplines have usually been excluded from any meaningful role in the evaluation process, they retaliate by fouling up the system. As long as their man has room to move within the assigned salary range, they appear to be content. But let him begin to close in on the maximum and the switchboard in the compensation department will light up. "I have assigned Sam some significant additional responsibilities in the last few months and I think that you should reevaluate his position. Obviously, it merits a grade 14 and not the grade 12 which it is currently assigned." If the manager gets his way, it won't be long before managers in other departments hear of this success story and begin to place their own form of pressure on the compensation group.

The point-factor approach also appears somewhat dishonest intellectually. The conscientious compensation analyst will confess that he is often astounded at the results produced by thoroughly objective evaluations made with the company's point-factor plan. "Why, that position can't be in grade 21," he says to himself, "it just has to be in grade 23." So he pulls down the shades, shuts the door, and "massages" his factor evaluations once again. After concluding that the position really requires a master's degree and not the bachelor's degree which he has assigned it, and that it calls for seven years of experience rather than the five he has assigned it, he manages—very scientifically, mind you— to evaluate the position into salary grade 23, *where it belongs.* Few individuals in the compensation field can deny having done the same thing—many times.

The Marketplace System of Position Evaluation

The marketplace appears to be a curious evaluator of executive positions—curious because the values the marketplace assigns to positions often differ wildly from those produced by most point-factor plans. But the marketplace is actually a wise evaluator.

During the Depression, the highest paid discipline was marketing, which made a lot of sense then because business's main objective was to sell products to people who couldn't afford them and who were, to say the least, uninterested. During and shortly after World War II, the production man came into vogue because in those days business's primary goal was to produce goods—whatever they were, and whatever the price, they could easily be sold. Today, the financial man is in his prime, what with the trend toward asset management.

A company can, of course, pay anything it wants to for a given position, but not even the largest of companies, General Motors and American Telephone, are big enough to make the market in executive compensation. Ultimately, *a position is worth what the market says it is worth.* No amount of temporizing or rationalizing will alter this simple fact. Comments such as "computer personnel are overpaid" are based on someone's subjective impression of equity, are largely self-serving, and do no one any good. True, in the next world where equity is perfect, computer personnel will surely be paid less; but we are operating in this world, and the fact is that computer personnel are not overpaid but are paid what they are worth. Who says so? The marketplace says so!

The concept of letting the marketplace arbitrate the question of a position's worth is central to the second major method of position evaluation used widely by companies today.

The marketplace method of position evaluation consists of six basic steps. The first involves the selection of a number of benchmark positions. As noted earlier, these are selected for their commonality with positions at competitor firms and for their representativeness as well.

For survey purposes, the next step is to select a number of competitor firms. A survey of the going rates paid the incumbents of these benchmark positions is the third step in the evaluation process.

The fourth step involves the design of a compensation structure to cover the positions that are to be evaluated. Taken alone, a compensation structure is nothing more than a series of numbers. It is obviously incomplete until the positions are actually assigned to various grades. Nevertheless, the distance from one point in a range to the same point in the next higher and lower ranges and the width of each range are significant and are built into the compensation structure design.

The fifth step is to place the benchmark positions in the compensation structure in accordance with their market worth.

The sixth and last step is to incorporate all the remaining positions into the structure based on a comparison of their duties and responsibilities with those of the benchmark positions whose market value is known and whose compensation grades have already been determined.

Let us now turn to a more detailed examination of each of the six steps.

Determining the Number of Benchmarks

How many benchmark positions should the company select for survey purposes? The answer to this question is governed by pragmatic rather than theoretical considerations, since the number of potential benchmarks (that is, positions whose mix of duties and responsibilities is common to many companies) is typically much larger than the number that can actually be used. The fact is that compensation personnel in the companies to be surveyed simply will refuse to tolerate a survey with an inordinately large number of benchmark positions. The resistance to participation in a survey generally rises with the square of the number of positions included in the survey, and the point of no return is reached around the 30-position level. Beyond that point, a company is likely either to refuse to participate or to give the survey short shrift, such that the gains in quantity of responses will be offset by a loss in quality.

Preparing the Survey Questionnaire

Having selected the benchmark positions, next we must prepare the survey questionnaire. The detail that this questionnaire should contain is partially dependent on whether the survey is to be conducted by mail or by personal visits to the participating companies. Time and money permitting, there is no question that personal visits are far better for producing high-quality data—and especially for controlling for comparability (the correct matching of positions on the basis of duties and responsibilities).

The survey questionnaire is essentially divided into two parts. The first part seeks general information on the company and the types of compensation plans it has. Since most of this information can be derived from published data, this part of the questionnaire serves as a checklist for materials to be obtained, such as annual reports, proxy statements, organization charts, copies of incentive compensation plan and stock option plan texts, and copies of group insurance, profit-sharing, savings, and retirement plans.

The second part of the questionnaire is devoted to a survey of the benchmark positions. A position description must be prepared for each position; its length depends on whether the survey is to be conducted by mail or by personal visits. If the latter approach is being utilized, a "capsule" position description will suffice—one of three or four sentences which sets forth only the major responsibilities of the position and in effect captures its essence. If more details are required to facilitate position matching, these can be readily provided during the personal interview.

A data sheet for each position is included in the questionnaire to elicit compensation and position scope information. Typical compensation data being sought include:

- Number of incumbents.
- Formal range of base salaries, if any.
- Range of actual base salaries, if there are two or more incumbents.
- Actual average salary.
- Incentive compensation awards for the past two to three years, including date and amount of award (and range of awards if there are two or more position incumbents).
- Stock option data for each incumbent, including data of grant and option price per share.

Some conventional data techniques should be mentioned at this point. Base salaries are usually expressed in annual terms for executive personnel and at the rate in effect as of the date of the survey (rather than the W2 rate for the preceding year).

Incentive compensation awards, on the other hand, are expressed as the total amount accrued for the year in which the award was earned, rather than the year in which it was paid. Thus a bonus of $10,000 paid in February 1977 but attributable to 1976 performance is listed as a 1976 bonus. If the bonus is paid in five installments and the first installment is only $2,000 (or perhaps the entire bonus is being deferred until retirement), the amount to be reported is still $10,000; that is, the amount that was *earned* even if not yet paid. Thus the total cash compensation (base salary plus bonus) reported for a given incumbent often differs from his true cash flow compensation.

To obtain a realistic picture of stock option grants, data must be sought for at least the five-year period preceding the date of the survey. This is because stock options, unlike salaries and bonuses, are not necessarily granted every year. Although the granting pattern may be annual in some companies, at others the grants are made sporadically. Nevertheless, most companies with option plans have historically made a grant to a given executive at least once in any five-year period, since five years represented the maximum span of exercise permitted under qualified stock option plans. If the company utilizes a nonqualified plan with a different maximum span of exercise, option data should be sought for the particular period of exercise rather than for the five-year period.

Position Scope

Position scope information is vitally important in any executive compensation survey. As a company expands, it typically increases the number of lower-level personnel. On the other hand, the number of top executive personnel is likely to remain unchanged. But each executive's responsibilities are expanded. Thus, if the company doubles in size, there is still likely to be only one financial vice-president. He will have a tougher job, however.

There are numerous position scope measures that the compensation analyst should take into account. The most obvious and hence most popular measure is sales volume. Presumably the scope is greater for a financial vice president in a company with $2 billion of sales than for one in a company with $1 billion of sales.

But sales volume is certainly not the only measure of position scope. Others that come to mind include the following.

Assets. Isn't it reasonable to assume that the scope is greater for a financial vice president in a company with $2 billion of sales and $2 billion of assets than for one in a company with $2 billion of sales and only $1 billion of assets?

Number of employees supervised. Isn't it reasonable to assume that scope is greater for a division general manager who supervises 10,000 employees directly or through subordinates than for one who supervises only 5,000 employees?

Number of exempt employees supervised. Isn't it reasonable to assume that the scope is greater for a division general manager who supervises 5,000 exempt employees and 5,000 nonexempt employees than for one who supervises 2,000 exempt employees and 8,000 nonexempt employees? Both have the same number of employees, but assuming everyone is correctly classified, the one who supervises a greater number of exempt employees heads the more sophisticated organization.

Reporting level. Isn't it reasonable to assume that the scope is greater for a financial vice president who reports directly to the chairman and chief executive officer than for one who reports to the president and chief operating officer?

Board membership. Isn't it reasonable to assume that the scope is greater for a financial vice president who sits on the company's board of directors than for one who sits in his office awaiting news from the boardroom?

At this point, one may ask: Why take the time and go to the expense of conducting a survey? Why not make use of available published data? The answer is that the company should perform a custom-tailored survey as well as use available published data.

The marketplace method of position evaluation rests on a foundation of valid data on competitors' going rates. Published survey information unfortunately cannot provide a strong enough foundation, since position comparability is generally looser; the surveys are conducted by mail, thus allowing interpretive errors to creep in; and the mix of participating companies cannot be controlled. As a result, the company may receive some information on its competitors by using a published survey, but it may also receive information that it doesn't want and that distorts the overall survey figures.

On the other hand, the value of published survey information should not be discounted entirely, because it is based on a much larger sampling of companies than any single company could easily obtain and hence contains a good degree of year-to-year reliability. This information therefore should be used when compiling market-place statistics for evaluation.

Picking the Survey Participants

While the company is preparing its survey questionnaire, it should also be deciding on the companies it wishes to have participate. Generally, there should be no fewer than 15 such companies, since with a smaller number one company may have too great an influence on the overall survey results. From a practical standpoint, the maximum number should be about 30.

The companies selected for participation should represent a good cross-section of the surveying company's competition. This means that both *product* competitors (those with which the company competes for sales) and *people* competitors (those with which the company competes for people) should be included. Particularly important are *double threat* competitors that compete for both products and people.

Selecting a company for a survey and getting it to participate are two different things. Resistance, however, is never as high as most people think, because compensation practices are relative, not absolute, so all companies have to depend on other companies to validate their own compensation practices. Nevertheless, a company is likely to find few takers unless it offers a summary of the findings to the participating companies so that they can get something in return for what they have given. The summary usually keeps company identities confidential (Company A, Company B, and so on) so that none of the participating companies can identify which response belongs to which company.

In this regard, considerable care must be taken to insure that the summary is indeed confidential, for there are many ways to break the code. For example, corporate sales, when used as a position scope variable, are a dead giveaway to anyone with a copy of the *Fortune* 500 list. Similarly, dates of option grants and option prices can be traced through published stock market data.

One further point should be mentioned with regard to selecting the survey participants. It is best that all have the same bonus practices as the surveying company now has or is about to adopt. That is, if the surveying company has a bonus plan (or is developing one), the participants should also have bonus plans. If the surveying company does not and will not have a bonus plan, then none of the participants should have a plan. (Of course, some absolutely key competitors with practices different from those of the surveying company may simply have to be included.) The reason is that base salary practices of bonus-paying companies differ from those of non-bonus-paying companies. More is said of this shortly.

It is also worth emphasizing that in any survey, position comparability is the independent variable and compensation is the dependent variable. That the reverse sometimes occurs can be illustrated by one experience of a compensation specialist. The compensation director of another company invited him to participate in a survey a number of years ago, and he accepted. The director indicated that this survey would feature very closely controlled position comparability and that as a result he would send the specialist detailed position descriptions in advance and then follow up with a personal interview. The specialist read the position descriptions, and when the director arrived they began to exchange data. The director started with the first position and proceeded to amplify on the written position description to be sure the specialist understood exactly what the position was all about. The specialist replied that his company had an identical position and explained all its duties and responsibilities. The director said, "That's perfect. Now, we pay our position $20,000 per year. What do you pay?" "We pay $15,000 per year," the specialist answered. There was a long pause. "Well," he said, "don't you have a higher-level position that pays around $20,000 per year?" In effect, he was looking for confirmation of his company's current practices; and if this required that position comparability be bent a little, so be it!

In the same regard, one must exercise care in selecting proper survey participants. All too often, the question is implicitly and insidiously transformed from "What do our competitors pay?" to "What do high-paying companies pay?" So the chief executive officer reads *Business Week*'s annual roundup of executive compensation levels, learns who's getting what, and calls his compensation director: "Say, about that survey you're about to conduct, I'd like to suggest three companies I think you would do well to include." The compensation director may be puzzled as to why a steel company like his should be interested in knowing what companies in consumer package goods, drugs, and computers are paying. He would be less puzzled, though perhaps more cynical, if he were to read the same issue of *Business Week* and see that the CEOs in these companies were heading the latest hit parade of executive pay.

Establishing Market Worth

After the survey is completed, the next step is to analyze the data and determine the correct going rates of base salary and total cash compensation to be used for evaluation purposes. Before doing so, however, the company should consider whether there is a need for adjustment of survey data to reflect the movement in market rates between the time the information was first reported and the current date. Such a course of action will probably be required only if a relatively long time span (six months or more) intervened between the time the first company was visited and the time the survey was completed. It is more likely that it will be required only with the supplementary published survey data, because such data usually contain a considerable time lag.

The percentage to be applied for this purpose should be conservative. If, for example, it is believed that compensation rates have been increasing lately at the rate of 8 percent per year, then a 7 percent annual rate of escalation should be adopted.

Three techniques can be used to analyze the survey data. The first employs simple descriptive statistics, the second is based on single correlation, and the third uses multiple regression.

Descriptive analyses. Descriptive techniques consist of the calculation of medians or averages and are useful when position scope is not a relevant factor: that is, when virtually all the positions have essentially the same position scope. Three averaging techniques may be employed.

The first is a simple unweighted average where each company's compensation information for a given position is added together, and the resulting figure is divided by the number of companies in the survey. Although it seems obvious, the surveying company should never include its own information in compiling going rates. For some reason, this mistake is frequently made. The surveying company's own information should, however, be used in preparing the summary for the participating companies.

The second average, which is weighted by population, is useful when there are multiple incumbents for each company's position. Each company's average compensation for that position is multiplied by the number of people holding that position, and then the resulting figures are added together and the sum is divided by the total population of all the companies.

A third technique, which is rarely used but can be extremely valuable, is to calculate a judgmental average. Essentially, the first average described—the unweighted average—does carry some implicit weights. In effect, if there are ten companies in the survey and an unweighted average is employed, each company is implicitly being assigned 10 percent of the total weight. This may or may not be an accurate representation. Perhaps one or two companies pose a particularly competitive threat to the surveying company; and one or two others, while still important, are less of a threat. If such is the case, a judgmental average can be useful.

The analyst first determines the average weight per company by dividing the number of companies into 100 percent. He then increases this average weight for the more important companies and decreases it for the less important companies such that the total always remains 100 percent. He then multiplies each company's compensation data by its assigned weight, adds the resulting figures, and divides by 100.

When used in connection with an unweighted average, the judgmental average provides a good indication of the influence that the most and least important companies are having on the overall going rates. This approach is also especially valuable in that the weighting patterns can be changed from position to position to reflect the fact that a given competitor does not pose the same threat in every situation. For example, a people competitor may be given a very high weighting on EDP executives because the market for these individuals transcends industry lines, and a company that can offer employment without physical transfer is bound to be a bigger threat than one that requires a 2,000-mile relocation. On another position, however, the same competitor may receive a very low weighting because incumbents are rarely observed to cross industry lines.

Single correlation. It is worth recalling that the primary purpose of any compensation survey is to determine why one executive makes more than another. When the compensation analyst decided to restrict his comparisons to positions having the same basic duties and responsibilities, he assumed that the duties and responsibilities of a particular position have a lot to do with the pay for that position. But suppose that even after holding duties and responsibilities constant, his descriptive statistics show a large variation in pay. The compensation analyst may be comforted to know that the average salary for financial vice presidents is $90,000. But what if he also discovers that the *range* for financial vice presidents in the survey is $60,000 to $175,000? Holding duties and responsibilities constant was of some help, of course, because executives in positions paying less than $60,000 or more than $175,000 dropped out of the comparison. Yet the remaining variation in pay is so large as to make him wonder whether $90,000 is the correct going rate for his financial vice president's position.

It is at this point that the technique of single correlation may prove helpful. Perhaps the compensation analyst noted that the sales volumes of the 30 companies in the survey range from $500 million to $3.5 billion. He may therefore hypothesize that the larger companies are paying their financial vice presidents near the upper end of the range and that the smaller companies are paying their financial vice presidents near the lower end of the range.

To test this hypothesis, the compensation analyst can feed the sales volume and pay information of the 30 financial vice presidents into a computer and have it determine the degree to which the dependent variable of pay is influenced by a change in the independent variable of sales volume. The end result is a mathematical formula which can graphically depict the relationship between sales volume and pay. Figure 1 illustrates such an approach.

Figure I. Typical organization sales/executive compensation curve.

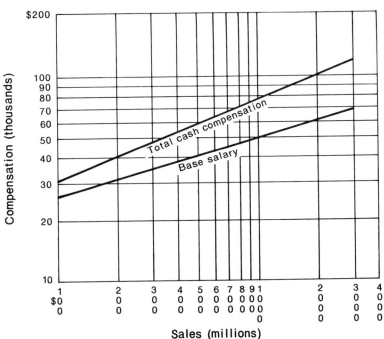

The going rate for the surveying company's position is read from the curve by referring to the organizational sales for which the surveying company's position is responsible. If desired, this going rate can be judgmentally averaged with similar curve information from published surveys. Obviously, the greatest weight should be placed on the custom-tailored curve.

In analyzing the data from a single correlation study, the compensation analyst should look not only at the trend line but, more important, at the *scatter* around the trend line. If the relationship between a change in sales volume and a change in pay were perfect, every individual data plot would lie on the trend line. But such is almost never the case. Thus there may be some correlation between sales volume and pay, but the correlation is likely to be far from perfect. Perhaps when he examines the scatter around the trend line, the compensation analyst will discover that he has narrowed the range of pay for financial vice presidents to $80,000 to $120,000 at the level of sales volume applicable to his company. But he has a sizable variance that he is as yet unable to explain, and he is not entirely sure of the going rate for his financial vice president.

That being the case, he can perform other single correlation studies. For example, he can test the relationship between assets and pay, or between number of employees supervised and pay. Perhaps he will find a better correlation and therefore a better explanation of why one financial vice president is earning more than another in the survey group.

Multiple regression. In a way, performing a single correlation study is akin to being a blind man who tries to learn what an elephant looks like by feeling its right ear. The man receives some information, but not enough to be able to visualize the elephant.

Thus the compensation analyst may discover some relationship between sales volume and pay and some relationship between assets and pay and some relationship between number of employees supervised and pay and some relationship between reporting level and pay. But no single relationship may be all that good.

There are few cases of true synergy in the business world, the claims of conglomerators notwithstanding, but here is one of them. Mixing together several good relationships between different variables and pay will not uncommonly generate a single excellent relationship. This can be done with a technique called multiple regression. In effect, our compensation analyst throws all his hypotheses into the computer at once. The computer then seeks to derive a mathematical model or equation that draws on some or all of his hypotheses and in the process accounts for more of the variation in financial vice presidents' pay than could be accounted for by utilizing any single hypothesis alone.

Such an equation might look something like this:

Log of total cash compensation = 2.6053 + (0.507 × log of sales volume)
+ (0.332 × log of assets)
+ 1.505 × number of exempt
– employees supervised)
+ (1.799 × 1 if a member of the
board of directors; or × 0 if
not a member)
–(1.235 × 2 if the position reports
directly to the CEO; or × 3 if the
position is on the second level
subordinate to the CEO, etc.)

The compensation analyst can then produce a going rate of total cash compensation for his financial vice president by substituting into the equation the values appropriate to his company. Perhaps the indicated going rate will be shown to be $115,000 and the multiple regression model will be so successful in determining pay differences that the applicable range of pay around this $115,000 figure will be only $105,000 to $120,000.

Many years ago, physicians who spotted parasites on the skin of patients formulated the hypothesis that there was a relationship between the parasites and disease. They were proved right when the patients recovered following removal of the parasites. But other patients without visible parasites died. Then the microscope was invented, and physicians were able to see parasites that had until then been invisible. The identification of these parasites—called bacteria— led to the development of new treatments, and more patients were saved. But others with similar symptoms still died. It was not until the invention of the electron microscope that scientists were able to "see" viruses for the first time and hence prove the existence of a relationship between viruses and disease.

So it is with the analysis of compensation data. When we are limited to the naked eye and—in our analogy—use only descriptive statistics, we may not get the right answer. When we use a standard microscope and single correlation techniques, we may improve matters but still be off the mark. When finally we turn to the electron microscope and multiple regression techniques the result may not be perfect, but in most cases, it will give us the best available answer to the perennial question: Why is it that one executive makes more than another?

Designing the Compensation Structure

At this point, the survey has been completed, the data have been analyzed, and going rates of salary and total cash compensation have been computed. The next step is to design a compensation structure.

The practice at most companies is to design only a salary structure and then pay bonuses as a percentage of current base salaries. The danger in such a practice is that it may lead to a pyramiding of compensation such that the individual with an outstanding base salary receives an outstanding bonus percentage applied to his salary. Thus he has unwittingly been paid more than once for the same performance contributions.

For that reason, a total integrated compensation structure is preferred, with each range containing five points: (1) base salary minimum; (2) base salary control point; (3) base salary maximum; (4) total compensation control point; and (5) total compensation maximum. Of these five points, the two on which the entire structure is anchored are the base salary control point and the total compensation control point.

It was indicated earlier that companies with bonus plans or those about to adopt one should confine their surveys to other companies with bonus plans. The reason is that bonus-paying companies typically pay lower base salaries than non-bonus-paying companies. When bonuses are added, however, the total compensation is almost always higher. Thus we have a good example of the principle of risk versus reward.

If a company with a bonus plan surveyed some companies with no bonus plans, this would raise the average going salary rates for all companies combined. If the company then designed its salary structure around these higher going rates and added a bonus equal to the average of bonus-paying companies, the result would be needlessly high total compensation.

Base salary control points. The buildup of the compensation structure starts with what will eventually become the base salary control point. A number is picked to represent what will probably be the lowest going rate for any executive included in the structure. Then a series of additional numbers is generated, each higher than the preceding, until a number is reached that will be the highest going rate for any executive included in the structure. These numbers are generated exponentially, with each number a certain percentage higher than the preceding number.

The proper percentage spread between control points is a matter of considerable controversy in the compensation field. One school of thought maintains that the spread should be low (say, a uniform 5 percent escalation) so that the decision to evaluate a position one grade higher or lower than is initially recommended will cost the company very little. There are two problems connected with this approach. The number of compensation grades produced is usually very high, with the result that the structure may become administratively unwieldy. Moreover, if it is too easy to "give up" a grade, such an action will probably occur with discomforting frequency.

Therefore, it is preferable to employ a constantly escalating structure approach. Generally, the lowest control points will be about 6 to 7 percent apart, with the percentage increasing gradually to around 10 percent at the $30,000 to $35,000 salary control point level.

Total compensation control points. Now we have a stream of numbers which eventually will become base salary control points. The next step is to generate a stream of numbers which will eventually become total compensation control points. One approach is to assign positions to the structure solely on their base salary going rates and then establish an average bonus percentage for each position such that the summation of (1) the base salary control point and (2) the base salary control point times the average bonus percentage would equal the average total compensation derived for that position from the survey data analysis.

The problem is that the average bonus percentages for various positions contain variations which may have nothing to do with the position level but result from the relatively small sample sizes. Thus two executive positions have the same base salary control point, but the survey data show that one should earn an average bonus of 50 percent of base salary and the other an average bonus of 45 percent of base salary. Although the survey data show that these differences do exist, one would have a time of it trying to justify such an approach to the two executives involved!

Therefore, average bonus percentages must be smoothed—or normalized—before the total compensation control points can be generated. To do this, each bonus in the entire survey (regardless of position) is plotted as a percentage of salary against the corresponding base salary. Using the computer, a trend line is derived from the scatter diagram. Such a trend line from a survey of 150 companies can be plotted from the date given in Table 1. (The reason why the bonus as a percentage of salary increases with increasing salary is explained later.)

For each base salary control point, the appropriate bonus percentage is determined using the normalized bonus trend line. This percentage is then applied to the base salary control point, the resulting figure added to the base salary control point, and we have the total compensation control point. Thus, if a given base salary control point is $50,000 per year and the trend line shows a 29 percent bonus, the resulting total compensation control point for that base salary control point is $64,500 ($50,000 + [50,000 ×29%]).

At this stage, the company has a series of base salary control points and total compensation control points which insure that it will properly track the competition. That is to say, an average performer will receive an average base salary, and he will also receive an average bonus. His combined salary and bonus will also equal the competitive average total cash compensation.

Table 1. Annual bonus expressed as a percentage of base salary.

Base Salary	Bonus %
$ 30,000	15
40,000	21
50,000	29
60,000	33
70,000	37
80,000	39
90,000	42
100,000	43
110,000	44
120,000	45
130,000	46
140,000	47
150,000	48
200,000	50

Restricting Bonuses to Above-Average Performance

Do companies want to reward average performance at all? Some companies, for example, will object to paying any bonus to an executive whose performance is only average. "We want to pay bonuses only for outstanding performance," they will say. These companies have therefore adopted the implicit stance of making their base salary control points the equal of the average total compensation control points. In that way, the average performer receives a salary which equals the average total cash compensation paid by other companies. Theoretically, there is no necessity to pay this man a bonus unless and until his performance rises above the average. Although such an approach is seemingly appealing, it has two pitfalls.

First, it violates the principle of the greater the risk, the greater the reward. To illustrate, let us assume that our survey shows a given position carrying an average base salary of $40,000, average total cash compensation of $50,000 (thus a 25 percent bonus), and maximum total compensation of $60,000 (that is, the highest-paid individual in this position typically receives $60,000 per year). The concept of paying salaries equal to average total cash compensation presents no problem when the executive's performance is average, but there is a significant problem when his performance is below average, above average, or outstanding.

If, for example, our hypothetical executive received an outstanding performance rating, he would, under the system used by some companies, receive a $50,000 base salary (equal to average total cash compensation) and a $10,000 bonus. His total compensation would therefore equal the maximum total compensation presumably paid to outstanding performers at other companies. The figures are right, but our hypothetical executive got a pretty good deal! He received the same total reward as his outstanding counterparts at other companies but he took less risk because his salary, representing assured income, was $10,000 higher per year. Similarly, if the executive's performance is below average, and he therefore receives no bonus, he still earns $10,000 more than his equally inefficient counterparts at competing firms. For that reason, establishing base salary control points to equal average total cash compensation should be avoided.

Another factor to consider in this regard is that, for reasons discussed later, most companies do not confine their bonuses to cases of outstanding performance but give virtually every executive a bonus each year. This applies not only to companies that pay bonuses for average performance but also to companies that say they pay bonuses only for outstanding performance. Thus the company that establishes its base salary control points to equal average total cash compensation is likely to pay awards even to its average performers. The result is a pyramiding of compensation that costs the company money but gives it little or nothing in return.

Paying Above-Average Compensation as a Matter of Policy

Another group of companies will reject the base salary control points and total cash compensation control points generated in the manner just described because, as they put it, "Our policy is to pay above average compensation. Therefore, the control points should be increased by 10 percent [or some such figure]." Such an argument is generally without merit. No company should ever pay more than others for average performance. The only possible benefit to be derived is an increased ability to hold average performers, and, statistically speaking, these are not hard to find in the event that turnover does increase. All the company does is greatly, and needlessly, increase its compensation costs.

The only time a company's aggregate compensation costs should be above the average of its competitors is when its mix of excellence is also above the average of its competitors. And this should be verified by referring to hard financial performance figures.

Creating More Reward Through Increased Risk

There is an alternative approach which does have merit and can be adopted by the gutty company. It is to decrease the base salary control points and increase the total compensation control points. The risk-reward principle dictates, however, that the exchange ratio be somewhat higher than one dollar of increased bonus opportunity for one dollar of decreased salary opportunity. As a rule of thumb, this approach should employ a two-for-one principle. To illustrate, let us assume once again that the competitors' average base salary is $40,000 per year for a given position and that their average total cash compensation is $50,000 per year. Let us further assume that those are the control points developed in the manner just described. A company could, if it desired, decrease the base salary control point by 10 percent—or $4,000 per year in this instance. Using the two-for-one principle, the total compensation control point would be increased by $4,000, such that the new base salary control point and the new total cash compensation control point would be $36,000 and $54,000 per year, respectively. (Thus, base salary potential dropped $4,000—from $40,000 to $36,000—while bonus potential increased $8,000—from $10,000 to $18,000.)

This approach can help the company reduce its fixed costs and keep its total compensation payments more in line with its ability to pay. It also offers the individual executive an opportunity to receive total compensation which is substantially in excess of industry levels at performance levels of average or above. But the individual executive also takes a risk, in that if his performance is poorer than average, he will receive total compensation (in this case a salary alone) which is less than that provided by the competition.

However, the larger the award opportunities, the stronger must be the company's performance appraisal infrastructure. And the company must be more willing to employ this infrastructure in making gutty performance assessments. Without these factors, the use of below average base salary control points and above average total compensation control points is a waste of time.

Companies contemplating this high-risk/high-reward approach should also be careful not to foul up their executives' life insurance coverage and pension opportunities. For example, many company pension plans predicate the resulting benefit on final average base salary, not final average total compensation. Hence the company that decides to inject more risk by reducing base salary may unwittingly pyramid that risk by reducing pension levels as well. This is not an insoluble problem—pension supplements can be designed—but it should not be overlooked.

Mention should be made here of the principle of salary "discounting." People have said that base salary control points established to equal something less than average total compensation represent a discounted salary structure. This is not an automatic case of discounting, since the base salary control points may still equal the average base salaries paid by other companies with bonus plans. It is preferable to restrict the term "discount" to the approach described previously where base salary control points are actually reduced below the level of average base salaries paid by other companies with bonus plans.

Establishing Minimum and Maximum Range Points

Let us assume that the company has decided to adopt conventional base salary and total compensation control points. The next task is to determine the base salary minimum and maximum points and the total compensation maximum point.

These figures can be derived from the salary and total compensation dispersion observed in the survey. If this survey is typical, it will show that the dispersion around the mean is somewhat asymmetrical. Thus the dispersion below the average runs out of gas (or goes spurious) at about 80 percent of the average figure. Above the average, however, this does not occur until about 130 percent of the average figure. This 130 percent guideline applies to both salary and total compensation frequency distributions.

One approach, then, is to derive the remaining three range points in the following manner:

1. Base salary minimum—80 percent of the base salary control point.
2. Base salary maximum—130 percent of the base salary control point.
3. Total compensation maximum—130 percent of the total compensation control point.

The first and third of these figures present no problem but the second does: Where should the above average to outstanding performer look for his rewards? To his base salary *and* his bonus? Or to his bonus alone?

A logical answer is that the great bulk of rewards for above average to outstanding performance should be placed in the bonus, because such an approach offers potentially more motivation. Therefore, the base salary maximum points could be reduced below what the survey would justify (say, 110–120 percent of the base salary control points), and, using the two-for-one principle, the amount of the decrease could be doubled and added to the total compensation maximum points.

This approach presents the danger of drastically overcompensating the outstanding performer. This is not cause for much concern, however, because, as noted earlier, one of the objectives of any sound compensation program should be to reduce turnover among the company's outstanding executives (rather than simply reduce total turnover).

In the field of psychology there is a concept known as cognitive dissonance, and some psychologists advocate that it be applied to compensation. The theory is that if an individual is deliberately overpaid, he will perceive a dissonance between his position and performance on the one hand and his compensation on the other. Since this may cause him to feel guilty, he will redouble his efforts to bring his performance into line with his compensation, thereby removing the source of dissonance. Perhaps an outstanding performer who is paid substantially more than outstanding performers in other companies will, because of his perceived dissonance, make an even greater performance contribution. (Who wouldn't like to volunteer as a subject for the first experimental application of the cognitive dissonance theory?)

Evaluating the Benchmark Positions

Our compensation structure has now been developed, so we can move on to the placement within this structure of the benchmark positions. The task is basically simple: Each position is placed in the compensation grade whose total compensation control point closely approximates the going rate of total compensation for that position.

Two points should be made here. First, the placement of positions into the structure theoretically could be accomplished either on a base salary control point basis or on a total compensation control point basis. Remember, however, that the distance between the base salary and total compensation control points was established through the use of a normalized bonus curve. Therefore, it is possible that the total compensation control point on certain positions would deviate from the going rate of total compensation as established by the survey, if the base salary control point were used for evaluation. Of course, the reverse can also occur, but it is of less significance because, by using the total compensation control point for evaluation, the company is assured that at least in this most important facet of compensation it is fully competitive.

Second, the question arises as to what to do when the competitor's going rate of total compensation lies between two total compensation control points. One approach is simply to round off—up or down as the case may be. In practice, however, some judgment and a good deal of negotiation will be required. More often than not, most positions will be rounded off to the next *higher* grade. Since the distance between one control point and another is never very great, however, this should not present any real problems.

Slotting the Nonbenchmark Positions

The last remaining task in developing the compensation structure is the evaluation of the nonbenchmark positions. Here is where the management gets deeply involved. And here is where the marketplace method of position evaluation pays off in terms of acceptance by line management.

Although some compensation experts will take issue, the supervisor of a position being considered for evaluation knows more about that position than anyone in personnel. Therefore, the task is to display the benchmark positions in chart form and enter into negotiations with line management on the slotting of the nonbenchmark positions. The word "negotiation" is not used carelessly, for that is ultimately what the slotting process involves. The compensation head does not merely write orders, but then again he is not a judge and jury either. The same applies to the line managers on the other side of the table.

With the chart there for everyone to see, one nonbenchmark position at a time is considered for evaluation. The position is viewed as a whole (taking all its duties and responsibilities together) and is compared to the applicable benchmark positions. Since these positions, if they have been selected properly, cover the entire spectrum of the positions to be evaluated—both vertically and horizontally—the process is essentially one of interpolation and fortunately not of extrapolation. Thus, after some discussion, agreement will usually be reached to the effect that a nonbenchmark position, in terms of duties and responsibilities, lies somewhere between two benchmark positions. After some further discussion and "fine-tuning," the proper grade is finally determined.

This process sounds and *is* rather unscientific. As the president of one firm put it, "All systems of position evaluation essentially boil down to organized rationalization." Remember that the point-factor method, for all its supposed accuracy, is just as unscientific and is also fraught with other problems that have already been discussed.

One helpful technique has been to portray the benchmark positions spatially but without the actual compensation ranges showing. When a line manager can see the ranges, his judgment as to the location of a nonbenchmark position is often clouded by his desire to see that the compensation of the current incumbent doesn't end up above the range maximum.

After the slotting process has been completed and all departments and divisions have had their "day in court," the last step is for the president (or the head of the particular unit) to review the entire structure, looking across disciplinary and divisional lines to insure that equity has been achieved both horizontally and vertically. As a result, some additional fine-tuning may occur, and certain positions may be raised or lowered one grade to conform with the evaluations assigned to comparable positions in different departments or divisions.

Internal mathematical modeling. An additional and valuable technique that can be used in position slotting is internal mathematical modeling. In effect, the company starts with a single dependent variable—in this case, the tentative base salary control point assigned to each position—and then selects a number of independent variables that it believes ought to have a bearing on the assignment of a higher base salary control point to one executive than to another. These independent variables can include the position's reporting level, the number of levels reporting to it, the number of exempt and/or total employees in subordinate organizational segments, the functional discipline involved, the education and experience required to perform the position, and so on. The computer is then instructed to perform another multiple regression analysis. With the results of this analysis, the company can

- See which of the independent variables actually has an influence on the tentative base salary control points.
- See the weighting that each variable has in the overall outcome.
- See the weighting that all usable variables have in combination.
- Identify those base salary control points that seem particularly out of line.

With this information the company can make changes in base salary control points, where appropriate, and then run further internal mathematical models to determine whether the changes helped to improve internal equity.

Adjusting the Structure

We now have what we know to be a viable compensation structure, one which by definition is externally competitive and, through the nonbenchmark slotting process, is internally equitable. But unless the structure is adjusted periodically, it will soon lose its competitive edge.

How often should the structure be adjusted? Certainly not more than once a year (unless our inflation rate approaches that of Brazil).

In addressing the problem of compensation structure escalation, a company using the marketplace method of position evaluation should adopt a conservative stance, recognizing that the market worth of certain positions moves at a faster rate than others (for example, EDP personnel).

The first step is to ascertain what the trend has been in executive salary escalation over the past year. Here is where published survey data can be of help, by enabling the company to see what several thousand companies have done as well as what the year-to-year trend is by industry. Sources could include AMA's Executive Compensation Service, occasional reports in the business press (such as the ones offered by *Business Week* each year), and data published by the Bureau of Labor Statistics (although these are mainly concerned with the salaries of lower-level personnel and thus will be of only indirect assistance). Still other sources include private surveys in which the firm has participated.

If all these sources make it apparent that executive salaries have increased approximately 8 to 9 percent during the year, the conservative company could then decide to escalate all five points in each range by 8 percent.

Next, the company must determine whether the going rates for any specific positions have moved at a significantly faster pace than 8 percent. Suppose there is good evidence that the market worth of the EDP executive's position has increased 12 percent during the past year. The company should then increase the current base salary control point of this executive's position by 12 percent (before adjusting for the 8 percent general escalation factor). This figure is then compared to the new base salary control points after the overall adjustment of 8 percent has been applied. If, on this basis, a one-grade increase appears desirable, such a course of action could be taken. And if it were taken, those nonbenchmark positions anchored to the EDP executive's position would also be considered for possible reevaluation.

Suppose that the increase in the EDP executive's going rate is not sufficient to justify a one-grade increase at this time. A record should then be kept of the proper new going rate; and next year, if the market worth for this position continues to increase at a faster pace than for other positions, the new escalation percentage could be applied to last year's proper going rate to determine whether a one-grade increase should finally be made.

Adopting a conservative stance in structure escalation minimizes the necessity of downgrading positions.

Using the Consumer Price Index

Throughout this discussion, changes in the market values of various positions have been used as anchor points in deciding on an appropriate salary structure adjustment percentage. But what about changes in the Consumer Price Index? In these inflationary times, many company managements, and most employees, instinctively believe that the salary structure adjustment percentage should be at least as high as the increase in cost of living and hopefully even higher. Their beliefs, though understandable, are ill-founded.

In more normal times, when inflation is low and worker productivity is increasing, the market value of most positions increases substantially faster than the cost of living does. If this were not so, today we would be enjoying—perhaps more accurately, not enjoying—the same standard of living as our ancestors experienced in 1776.

When inflation begins to surge, the market value of various positions typically increases at a faster rate than before, but it does not necessarily continue to outpace that of the cost of living. In fact, there have been years in the very recent past when job market values barely managed to keep pace with cost of living. And there was one year when inflation surged 12%, while job market values managed only a 9% gain. In that case, *real* income decreased.

Accordingly, it makes sound economic sense to ignore changes in the cost of living when deciding upon salary structure adjustment percentages. If job market values increase faster than the cost of living, so be it. But even if they don't, so be it. By definition, such an approach keeps one even with one's competitors, and that, after all, is the underlying objective of the exercise. Given our generally rising standard of living, in most years employees will come out ahead, though they may lose purchasing power in some years. Those companies that have taken the time to explain these economic facts of life to their employees have generally found a surprisingly understanding audience.

After adjusting the structure and acting on any market worth anomalies caused by shifting supply and demand, the company should also consider whether certain positions should be upgraded (or downgraded) because they have undergone a significant change in position scope. For example, suppose two divisions have been consolidated into one and the position scope of the division manager, measured in terms of division sales, has increased from $100 million to $200 million. A recheck of the position scope graphs or multiple regression equations prepared earlier will determine how much of a reevaluation is required to reflect a change of this magnitude.

Because this method of compensation structure escalation is based on general industry trend information, it is of course subject to error. Therefore, a periodic resurvey of some, if not all, of the original benchmark positions should be made and the structure adjusted to reflect current trends. In this manner, errors stemming from the use of trend information, which will be small in any event, can be corrected before they are compounded. A resurvey of this type should be undertaken every other year—or at least every third year.

By following the procedure just mentioned, a company will be assured that its compensation structure is up to date—at least as of the date the revisions are made. Of course, as the months roll by the structure may fall below the market. As a result, some companies add enough additional escalation to the structure to make it theoretically competitive in the middle of the year for which it will be effective, rather than at the beginning of the year. In this manner, the structure will lead the market slightly during the first six months and lag behind slightly during the last six months. There is nothing wrong with such an approach, because it inflates the structure only by one-half year's escalation—or perhaps 3 to 4 percent. Because it is so harmless, however, many other companies will say, "Why bother?" And there is nothing wrong with not bothering either.

Although much material has been discussed in this chapter, it all boils down to just a few basic points.

1. Use the marketplace method of position evaluation to save time, properly track the competition, and achieve the needed degree of internal equity.
2. Develop an integrated compensation structure which combines both base salary and total cash compensation progression.
3. Adopt compensation structure escalation procedures which insure that the structure continues to maintain the same competitiveness it had on the day it was first implemented.

Paying for Performance_____3

The compensation structure in its totality may be viewed as a giant plus sign. An individual executive moves up the vertical bar of the plus sign (from one control point to another) in accordance with the responsibilities assigned him. He moves across the horizontal bar of the plus sign (from base salary minimum to total compensation maximum) in accordance with his performance. We now turn our attention to the movement along the horizontal bar.

Making Use of the Learning Curve

Many companies have contented themselves with rather simple rules for determining the size of an increase an executive is to receive. As one company put it, "We give 10 percent for outstanding performance, 8 percent for above average performance, 6 percent for average performance and nothing for below average performance."

Such an approach neglects two important factors. First, the progress of human learning is uneven. Repeated psychological studies have demonstrated that all human learning—and increased performance on the job is essentially a matter of learning—follows a similar pattern: One learns a given task extremely rapidly at first and then begins to slow down over time. Eventually, the rate of learning peaks out and may even decline in some instances. Now, the way in which people learn is really rather logical, since if we don't know much to begin with, it is fairly easy to double our small store of knowledge in a short time. On the other hand, if we already know a great deal, it takes much longer to double our large store of knowledge.

If compensation is going to be used as a motivational tool, it must match the individual's performance. Since not all individuals perform in the same manner, matching compensation to performance means that some will get a lot more than others. Hence we have the basis for recognition. And it is recognition, especially at the executive level, that is highly motivating.

If compensation is going to match performance, then it obviously must match the learning curve. Unfortunately, however, too many companies fail to follow this principle. If an executive's performance is improving rapidly because he is on a new job and hence on the steep portion of his learning curve, he is still likely to get only a 10 percent increase at most. Later, when his performance has slowed down but is on a sustained high level, the 10 percent increase will still be coming along as regular as clockwork.

In a way, the compensation practices at these companies are comparable to an old cargo ship pulling out of New York harbor: The pace is terribly slow at first and not much faster later on, but eventually it gets you there. The trouble is that this approach opens a terrible compensation gap during the years when the individual is on the steep portion of his learning curve. He is moving at jet speed, while the company's compensation program chugs along at 15 knots. This gap is illustrated in Figure 2, wherein a typical company compensation curve is superimposed on the learning curve.

It is noted in this exhibit that the typical company compensation curve eventually crosses the learning curve, thereby creating a gap in the opposite direction. Obviously this doesn't happen in every case but the high incidence of overpaid executives is nonetheless discomforting. "I just can't understand how that guy can make so much money," is a comment often heard in company corridors. Indeed, the problem is such that it has been facetiously suggested more than once that the company should at least capitalize on its policies by telling its executives, "Stick with us long enough, and on the average, you'll receive the proper amount of compensation during your career with the company."

In today's highly competitive environment for executive talent, however, this is no solution. Those whom the company most wants to keep are the very ones who are likely to be lost unless the compensa-

Figure 2. Typical compensation progression versus typical learning curve.

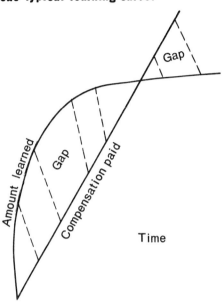

tion gap is closed. This happens because the steeper the learning curve, the better the performance and potential of the individual; and the steeper the learning curve, the wider the compensation gap is likely to be.

Establishing Compensation Targets for Varying Performance Levels

A second and related problem with the approach of granting a given percentage increase for a given performance level is that it fails to take into account the individual's current compensation position. Thus a man who is outstanding but whose earnings are only average will most likely receive the same 10 percent increase as the man who is outstanding but who is already earning an outstanding salary. In fact, the problem will be exacerbated because the percentage is applied to a much lower salary in the case of the first individual.

The proper amount of compensation increase, then, should be determined by the gap between where the individual is now and where he should be according to his performance contributions.

The concept is simple, but many companies consistently fail to apply it. In effect, it's as if a company's top executives and those whose compensation is being controlled are speaking two different languages. On the one hand, the top management, in response to compensation complaints, says, "What does the guy want? He's had two promotions in the past two years and we've given him the 10 percent maximum merit increase for as long as we can remember. He's come a long way fast, and he ought to be satisfied." The complaining manager, on the other hand, says, "I know I've come a long way fast, but I'm still way behind where I should be in terms of what I am supposed to do and the manner in which I'm doing it."

In a way, both these points of view are correct, but equity is on the side of the manager whose compensation is lagging behind his performance.

Such gaps can be closed by a simple stroke of the pen—certainly with much less trouble than the resolution of a personality conflict or some other intangible problem. Yet they continue to remain open. Top managers of companies with these problems are usually very pragmatic when it comes to negotiating with unions, because they really have no choice. And they are pragmatic when it comes to negotiating with a prospective executive who is employed by another company. Unless a satisfactory compensation package is offered, the executive will simply stay where he is or seek employment elsewhere. Yet once an individual joins the company and is not represented by a union, the top managers, for some inexplicable reason, assume that the rules of the marketplace do not apply. If a compensation problem develops, given enough time, they will solve it. More likely, one of their competitors will solve it for them.

Another irritating practice is to recognize the gap concept and the gap itself but refuse to do anything about it on the grounds that a big increase will spoil an executive and make him want the same treatment every year. Certainly the executive may want the same treatment every year—who wouldn't? But presumably he didn't get where he is without a certain degree of maturity, and therefore he should be capable of realizing that he can't remain on a steep learning curve forever. (A baby weighing 8 pounds at birth who continued gaining at his initial rate by doubling his weight every six months would weigh some 262 tons by the time he was eight years old!) There is far less risk in paying each executive what he is worth when he is worth it and taking the chance of having a few malcontents than in following the reverse procedure and insuring that there will be many malcontents—all excellent performers.

The proper and more motivationally rewarding policy that a company should follow is to establish targeted positions within the compensation range for various levels of performance. Since the base salary control point and the total compensation control point have been set to equal competitors' going rates, it follows that these are the targeted points for the average performer. Other targeted positions would include—

- *Base salary minimum and no bonus* for the new executive who is still not up to speed or for the poor performer.
- *Halfway between the base salary minimum and control points and no bonus* for the mediocre to marginal executive.
- *A combination of salary and bonus equal to an amount halfway between the total compensation control and maximum points* for the above average executive.
- *A combination of salary and bonus equal to an amount ranging up to the total compensation maximum point* for the truly outstanding performer.

Once these targeted positions are established, the merit increase is determined by computing the gap between the point in the range that the executive now occupies and the point he should occupy according to his performance assessment.

Closing Compensation Gaps

Theoretically all gaps, no matter how large, should be closed at once. From a practical standpoint, however, a company may wish to use some prudence. For example, salary gaps of 15 percent or less could be closed at once, and those of more than 15 percent could be closed in a series of more frequent but smaller increases, such that the gap becomes fully closed within a period of two years at the outside. Meanwhile, the bonus can be used to take up the slack.

Closing a compensation gap, however, requires the same ability to track the target as does shooting a duck, for a compensation gap is unlikely to remain static. First, the individual may still be improving his performance in his current position; thus, if his targeted position today is based on an assessment as an above average performer, it may well be based next year on an assessment as an outstanding performer.

Second, the range itself is escalating from year to year owing to commensurate escalation in going rates.

Third, the individual may well be promoted very soon. So, although his performance position in his new job may drop, he is in a higher range, thereby causing his dollar compensation gap to rise significantly.

Fourth, the individual may succeed in increasing the scope of the present position, thereby causing a reevaluation of the position and possibly a classification in a higher compensation grade. The result is identical to that of a bona fide promotion.

Thus, if the individual's current compensation gap is 20 percent, it may not remain so for long, and the company had better plan a string of, say, 15 percent increases to be granted at annual or even less frequent intervals to ensure that its tracking is correct and that the gap will be closed in the maximum two-year period.

Using Potential as a Compensation Factor

Looked at another way, the problem of tracking a moving gap is really one of estimating an executive's potential for future growth. Now, some will say that potential has no business being in a compensation program and that only current demonstrated performance should count. This is similar to saying that one can drive at 90 miles per hour whether the distance is 100 feet or 100 miles. To reassure the purists, the use of an executive's potential for tracking purposes in no way causes him to be overpaid at any time in terms of his current demonstrated performance. All that happens is that the current gap, which has nothing whatever to do with a man's potential, is closed at a faster rate if it is believed that future performance or position growth will not be long in coming.

Incorporating the concept of potential into the compensation system requires some care, however. To say that a man has potential is utterly devoid of meaning unless one knows the asnwers to two questions: Potential for what? Potential in what period of time? At a given point, an executive's potential to become say, a vice-president is obviously different from his potential to become president of the company. Moreover, his potential to become a vice-president in one year differs from his potential to make it in two years.

It seems that for compensation tracking purposes the prediction of potential for a period in excess of two years is too risky. Accordingly, the compensation planner should consider an executive's potential within this time frame and for various performance levels or new positions.

Handling Negative Gaps

Sometimes, of course, we are faced with a negative compensation gap, where the individual's current compensation exceeds his targeted range position. Obviously no action should be taken if the gap is small because periodic escalations in the compensation structure will remove the gap in a relatively short time—and because of the factor of standard error in performance appraisal.

On the other hand, large negative gaps (say 15 percent or more) may require a very unpalatable course of action: a salary decrease. This is especially the case if the company has been following the compensation gap philosophy in the past, because in that event a negative gap would be likely to stem only from a performance decline. In such a situation, the chances of a performance improvement are slim (unless the reasons for the decline are entirely external to the individual), but the chances of further decline are somewhat greater.

Using Compensation Ranges as Guidelines

Some executives react with horror at the thought of anyone's compensation going above the maximum of his range. (Compensation below the minimum is of course an indication of prudent management!) To them, the maximum is not a guideline but a concrete wall. Although their anxiety is understandable (having to abandon the safety of the average is bad enough but going above the maximum is ridiculous), they do their company a disservice by holding to their beliefs. For the maximum—at least as it has been designed in Chapter 2—*is* a guideline.

Remember that the minimum and the maximum range points were established to "cut off the tails" of the curve and eliminate the spurious portions of the frequency distribution. As such, these points represent approximately the 10th to the 90th percentiles of the distribution. Therefore, it is still possible—although admittedly improbable—for an individual to turn in a performance so superb as to justify paying him above the maximum of his assigned range. Albert Einstein would probably have qualified for such compensation treatment. Moreover, there is no reason why such an individual should not continue to receive still further increases.

The alternative to such an approach is to reevaluate the person's position and assign it a phony compensation grade. But this alternative may have repercussions on the evaluations of other positions in the organization, thereby increasing the company's potential compensation costs. Furthermore, when the superb performer finally leaves his position, he will probably not be replaced by someone equally superb; yet the unduly high compensation grade will probably not be lowered.

Consider, if you will, that paying compensation above the maximum represents the ultimate in recognition. What better way is there to motivate superb performance?

Timing the Increase

There is considerable disagreement in the compensation field as to when an individual should be reviewed for salary action. Some say annually on the individual's anniversary date (or some other date which staggers reviews throughout the year.) Some say annually on a department by department basis. Some say annually for everyone after the close of the year. Although there are pros and cons to each of these approaches, the last one mentioned seems preferable. It ties in with a performance appraisal system geared to the attainment of objectives, which, after all, are usually established on a fiscal-year basis. Having to review the performance of many executives at one time can be a drain on the reviewers and may therefore reduce the quality of appraisals, but a review system which randomly staggers increases throughout the year would lose its all-important motivational link with demonstrated performance.

Increases should be considered for times other than the annual review, however. For example, when a large compensation gap cannot be closed all at once, increases at six-month intervals can be usefully employed.

A case can also be made for giving an occasional spot increase to an executive who has demonstrated exceptional skill on a particular project. Such an increase, which would have to operate within the compensation gap principle and not create a negative gap, can be highly motivational simply because it is totally unexpected. Like investors in the stock market, executives anticipate what their regular merit increases will be and then "discount" future growth. When they receive the increase they anticipated, their short-term motivation, like the price of stock which has already been discounted, may not rise appreciably. On the other hand, an increase at an unexpected time can be enormously stimulating, especially when it comes immediately after the performance on which it is based and therefore increases the cause-and-effect relationship between rewards and performance that is at the motivational heart of any sound compensation program.

There are some companies that slow down the frequency of merit increases as the executive begins to near the maximum. Thus the executive is reviewed annually until he reaches the control point of his range; thereafter the review period is stretched to 18 months until he reaches a point halfway between the control point and the maximum. Then the review period moves to two years. These companies explain their policy through reference to the learning curve. As the individual's performance moves past the average mark his rate of growth necessarily slows down.

On its face, such an explanation makes sense. But these companies seem to want the best of both worlds, since there is little evidence that early salary progression is extremely fast because of the same learning curve principle. Moreover, these companies fail to use potential in tracking the executive's short-term progress over, say, the next two years. Viewed on this basis, the executive may be nowhere near running out of gas.

Slowing down the frequency of merit review is an acceptable— even desirable—policy when an executive shows signs of reaching the end of his *career* learning curve. Short of that, it is more of a disincentive ("congratulations, your performance is outstanding, and as a reward we are going to review you once every two years") and simply leads to the creation of a wider compensation gap.

The real reason why companies slow down the merit increase frequency is to prevent the individual from reaching the maximum and having no further room to move. As noted earlier, it seems far more desirable to work on closing compensation gaps than to worry about the dire motivational consequences that might ensue from paying a man what he is worth.

Publishing the Structure

After developing a viable compensation structure and intelligent rules for its use, the company must then concern itself with the effect the new structure's publication will have on its executives. Some executives balk at publishing their compensation structure and merit review guidelines because they feel it can only cause trouble. First, executives in certain disciplines will come to realize that they don't have as high an earnings potential as executives in other disciplines. Second, a man will put great pressure on the company if the rules say an outstanding individual is supposed to be at the maximum and he is outstanding but somewhere lower in his range. Third, there will also be pressure on the company to give everyone an increase at least equal to the amount of the annual structure escalation because not to do so would imply a performance decline under the review guidelines.

Let us consider these objections. First, to think that executives are not aware of interdisciplinary differences in market worth is to give them little credit for knowing what is going on in American business. Second, it is true that a man whose performance is considered outstanding but who is not at the maximum of his range will put pressure on the company to remedy the inequity, but why shouldn't he? Perhaps, by publishing the ranges and the accompanying guidelines, the company in some cases will be forced to call a spade a spade and tell an average executive that he is average, rather than buoy up his morale by giving him a false impression of his performance.

Third, it is also true that by not increasing an individual's salary at the same rate applied to the structure, a performance decline is implied. Yet the performance decline is not necessarily absolute but can be relative to the performance of other executives. Presumably, increases in the compensation structure reflect not only cost-of-living and supply-demand factors but also at least some amount of increased productivity. In the case of an executive, increased productivity doesn't necessarily mean that the job is getting done faster each year. Rather, it usually means that the knowledge and experience required to perform the job are steadily increasing as a function of increasing technology. Witness the computer, which has made the jobs of some managers easier but has greatly complicated the jobs of others—especially top managers. People who couldn't spell "operations research" and "linear programming" yesterday must now be able not only to spell them but to understand them. Thus today's mediocre manager would probably have been considered outstanding a decade or so ago; and today's outstanding manager will probably be considered mediocre in the next decade unless he continues to increase his "productivity."

Thus there is an ever increasing number of executives who, although doing as well as ever, are failing to keep up with the advance in technology and hence are falling behind when compared to their peers. Giving them increases which implicitly deny this fact would seem to be doing them a grave disservice over the long term.

It seems evident that the arguments against publishing the compensation structure and its guidelines are tenuous. On the other hand, there are some compelling arguments *for* publication. The most important is the opportunity that management has to make better use of the recognition principle. A man who reads the published material and observes that he is at the maximum of his range—or even above it —knows that his performance is outstanding and is being recognized. A man who reads the published material and observes that he is at the control point knows—despite the saccharine rhetoric of his boss—that he is only average; he probably knew it anyway. In short, if compensation motivates through recognition, why defeat these motivational purposes by shrouding the company's compensation policies in secrecy?

Publishing the compensation structure and its guidelines also has another salutary effect. It forces management to hew to its own policies. Compensation gaps are likely to be closed more quickly if everyone knows it is supposed to be done. Because of this, and because no company has unlimited funds to spend on increases, the number of individuals not receiving increases is likely to rise. Thus a new kind of compensation gap will be created—between outstanding and mediocre performers. That is the kind of gap that creates recognition and the motivation to achieve the company's corporate objectives.

Promotional Increases

One last item deserving of mention here is promotional increases. For some reason, a number of companies consistently refuse to grant promotional increases at the time of promotion. The increase follows either at the time of the next merit review or when "the man has proved he can do the job." This is a clear-cut violation of the risk versus reward principle. The executive is being asked to take a riskier job; he also must take more personal risks while he is learning how to function in his new position. Moreover, if management didn't already think he would be effective in the new position, it presumably wouldn't have offered him the promotion in the first place.

Increases should, if anything, be greater for promotions than for merit reviews, and they should always occur at the time the promotion is granted. An increase should take the executive at least to the minimum of his new range (no matter what percentage is required), because there is no valid reason for keeping anyone below the minimum. And, if there is reason to believe that the executive's performance will be more than minimal in a short time (say, six months), then he should be taken to the targeted range position applicable to that level of performance.

The motivational value of compensation can be increased by paying for performance through

1. Establishing targeted range positions for various levels of performance.
2. Using an executive's short-term potential to track his anticipated performance and position growth.
3. Adopting the compensation gap principle and a policy which aims at closing current gaps as soon as possible after they occur, but within no more than two years.
4. Publishing the compensation structure and its associated guidelines.
5. Granting meaningful increases at the time of the promotion.

The Annual Executive Bonus _____ 4

A company's annual bonus plan is potentially one of the two most important motivational elements in its entire compensation package. The key word here is "potentially"; unless certain design principles are followed, a bonus plan's potential will never be realized. Although most of these principles have been introduced earlier, it will be well to recapitulate here.

Basic Design Principles

First, the plan must be designed to stimulate behavior which leads to the attainment of the goals the company really wants to attain. We have seen that this design task requires a great deal of thought, because a company's real goals are not always what convention dictates.

Second, the plan should be extended only to those executives whose duties and responsibilities give them the opportunity to make a material and substantial impact (for good or ill) on the achievement of the goals. While it is true that every employee has some impact on the achievement of goals, it is equally true that few employees have a really *substantial* impact. It is these executives to whom the plan must be directed. This is not to say that special awards should not be given to the rare individual in a lower-level position who performs better than was ever expected.

Third, the plan should provide for payment of truly meaningful awards. Awards of one month's salary are ineffective. Bonuses will have to range upward of 50 to 60 percent at the highest levels in order to motivate. Moreoever, the bonuses should rise sharply as the company closes on its objectives to recognize that these last increments of performance are the hardest to achieve and at the same time are the most profitable.

Fourth, the plan should generally distinguish between the performance contributions of individual executives, offering some of them a maximum award and others a lesser award or even none at all.

Fifth, and finally, the plan will have to be revised and strengthened from time to time to overcome the inevitable erosion that most plans experience.

Eligibility

Determining who is and who is not eligible for the executive bonus plan is without a doubt the dirtiest job in the plan's design. It is easy to say that those whose duties and responsibilities offer them the opportunity to make a substantial impact on the attainment of goals should be eligible. The converse is also true: Those whose duties and responsibilities do not offer them the opportunity to make a substantial impact should be ineligible. But how does one distinguish between substantial and insubstantial impact when the responsibilities in any company are not discrete but overlapping and continuous, extending in an unbroken progression from the janitor to the president?

The fact is that wherever the line is drawn, the result is going to be at least somewhat arbitrary. Some companies have ducked behind titles and said that only officers are eligible to participate. This kind of selection causes a number of "statutory" officers (for example, an assistant secretary) to be included unnecessarily. Some companies have gone to the other extreme and declared that all exempt personnel are eligible, but this is merely ducking behind the Fair Labor Standards Act, in which definitions of exempt and nonexempt personnel are extremely arbitrary.

There is no easy answer, then, to the question of eligibility. But there are certain guidelines to use in this dirty job.

First, a distinction can be drawn between those whose responsibilities cause them to have a two-way impact on the attainment of goals and those whose responsibilities permit them to have only a one-way impact. To illustrate, if the decisions that some executives make turn sour, the result can be harmful to the company. Yet, if those decisions turn out to be wise, the results can be highly beneficial. Thus executives of this type have a two-way impact on the attainment of goals.

On the other hand, take the case of a dispatcher in a pipeline. His is a highly paid job, and he is responsible for the correct and timely movement of millions of gallons of oil products. If he makes the wrong decisions, his products may be contaminated, customers may receive the wrong delivery, or the pipeline may be completely stopped. Thus there is a lot riding on his successful performance. Yet, if this dispatcher makes all the right decisions, the best that can happen is that the company will not suffer. His is a job with only one-way impact. He can foul things up with a vengeance, but he can rarely make the company better than it already is.

There are many people in a company with one-way impact, but there are few with true two-way impact.

Another guideline is the practices of one's competitors, although obviously this should not be followed in a totally mechanistic fashion. Studies have shown that, as a company increases in size, the number of bonus eligibles also increases; however, the number of bonus eligibles as a percentage of the total company population decreases. This is as it should be, for doubling in size does not require doubling the number of key executives. Rather, a limited number of new key executive positions are created, and the current executives receive an increase in their position scope.

Generally speaking, large companies whose employees number 25,000 or more typically extend bonus eligibility to about 1 percent of their total population. Companies in the 5,000 to 25,000 size range usually extend bonus eligibility to 1 to 2 percent of their total population. These figures must be tempered by four considerations, however.

First, the percentage of bonus eligibles is generally higher in labor-intensive industries than in capital-intensive industries. In the latter group, fewer and more major decisions are made, often involving hundreds of millions of dollars at one time, and as a result few executives are entrusted with such decisions.

Second, the percentage of bonus eligibles is higher in companies with sophisticated technology than in companies making fairly mundane products. Although these companies cover about the same percentage of their exempt population as companies with less sophisticated technology, their coverage as a percentage of total population is higher because they have so many more exempt personnel.

Third, the percentage of bonus eligibles in decentralized companies with divisionalized organizational structures is generally higher than that in centralized companies. This is related to the earlier discussion of labor-intensive industries. In both situations, decision making is spread to more executives.

Fourth, the percentage of bonus eligibles is generally higher in the most successful companies than in the least successful companies. One study relating bonus eligibility percentages to returns on assets for 16 companies showed that the correlation was 0.6. Although one might conclude that the most successful companies got that way because they covered more people for bonus eligibility, it is more likely that they were better able to grant more awards.

Ultimately, the question of eligibility levels is decided pragmatically. A company can allocate only so much money to executive bonuses without angering the shareholders. Thus it usually faces a choice of having many eligibles and low awards or fewer eligibles and very meaningful awards. From a motivational standpoint, of course, there is no choice but the second alternative.

One approach to eligibility determination is to target a percentage of total population using the guidelines just mentioned, select the positions to be included, calculate the funds required, and consider whether the funding formula needed to produce these funds is excessive when compared to those of other companies.

Formal Eligibility Criteria

How should a company go about selecting the specific positions for bonus eligibility? Some companies develop definite eligibility criteria and let the chips fall where they may. These criteria usually involve four types of cutoffs.

1. Salary cutoff: anyone with a base salary of $30,000 or more per year is included.
2. Salary grade cutoff: anyone assigned to compensation grade 18 or above is included.
3. Organizational cutoff: anyone in the top two levels directly below the president is included.
4. Combination cutoffs: anyone in the top two levels of the organization who is also in compensation grade 16 or above is included, as is anyone in compensation grade 18 or above, regardless of organizational level.

Cutoff 4 is the best approach, because types 1 to 3, when taken individually, contain problems. Salary cutoffs discriminate in favor of disciplines with a high market worth and often result in some lower-paid executives with important responsibilities being crowded off the list. Salary cutoffs also interrupt the smooth flow of salary payments. For example, there seemed to be no good reason why one company had 200 executives at $24,999 per year until it was learned that the company's bonus cutoff was $25,000 per year.

Salary grade cutoffs present fewer problems than salary cutoffs but again are unduly influenced by the market worth considerations that went into the compensation structure design.

Organizational level cutoffs are too easily subject to political tampering and as a result sometimes lead to the inclusion of individuals with relatively minor responsibilities and the exclusion of individuals with truly major responsibilities.

Formal eligibility criteria should be established only after the fact and should be used to rationalize the eligibility selections that have already been made. This approach involves a critical examination of each executive position, from the top down. It will be readily apparent that some positions *must* be included. It will be just as apparent that other positions should not be included. And there will be a group of borderline positions. At this point, tentative decisions should be made on each borderline position. Then the designer should attempt to formulate eligibility criteria which include all the selections that have been made and exclude all other personnel in the company. Probably no set of simple yet meaningful criteria can be designed to do the job perfectly, and as a result some problem cases will crop up— a few eligibles who would be knocked off the list by the formal criteria and a few noneligibles who would be added to the list. Just as probably, these problem cases will all have been included in the original group of borderline eligibles. The company may well decide to accept these minor revisions dictated by the formal eligibility criteria. Used in this manner, such criteria impose a sort of discipline on the company and facilitate an optimum degree of internal equity.

Once these criteria have been drawn, deviations should *never* be permitted without a total redesign of the criteria themselves. Since the criteria break what was essentially a continuum of responsibilities and are therefore somewhat arbitrary, even one deviation can lead to the demise of the whole system.

To illustrate, a company decided to employ a status type of badge system. Supervisors were given red badges, and nonsupervisory exempt personnel were given candy-striped badges. The system was arbitrary, but as long as everyone understood how it worked there were no problems. One day a high-level engineering specialist who was not a supervisor turned up at the personnel director's office. "This system is ridiculous," he complained. "Here I am in a very important job earning three times what those foremen in the factory earn, and they look down their noses at me because they have a red badge and I have a candy-striped one. I can't get my job done without a red badge!"

The personnel director made what turned out to be a fatal decision: He agreed to give the engineer a red badge. Of course, once he received his new badge, the engineer ran as fast as he could to his work group and began to flaunt his new status symbol. Naturally, engineers made the trip to the personnel office in a steady stream. "We understood the system before," they said, "but if Joe is going to have a red badge, we have to have one also." They too received red badges and were then followed by individuals in other disciplines who heard what good results could be obtained from a visit to the personnel office. Pretty soon, there were so many red badges around that the candy-striped badges became status symbols in their own right.

Eventually, the company had to eliminate the whole program and substitute a uniform badge for all exempt personnel, thereby losing the status advantages of the previous system. By the same token, a company which deviates from its arbitrary rules governing bonus eligibility is going to be faced with the same problem.

Informing an Executive of His Eligibility

Once the eligibility rules have been established, people who are eligible should be informed. In effect, they should be told that they will receive an award each year or be given the reasons for not receiving one. Informing the individual of his eligibility has two advantages. First, it motivates him to go after the prize. In short, it puts the carrot in front of the horse rather than behind it. Second, it gives him considerable status in the eyes of his associates. Status is just another word for recognition, and recognition is a motivator.

Of course, such an approach may create some dissatisfaction among those who didn't make the eligibility list. But at least it clears up a question in many executives' minds: "Was I considered for an award and found lacking, or was I not considered at all?"

Special Awards

As noted earlier, the company should also provide special, one-shot awards to personnel not regularly eligible to participate. On rare occasions, an individual in a lower-level position makes an unexpected contribution which *does* have a very significant impact on the company's success. Examples of these types of contributions are an engineer who achieves a vital technological breakthrough and a purchasing agent who discovers a way to save the company a million dollars.

By definition, such contributions are not going to occur very often, and it is highly unlikely that the same individual will turn in performance of this magnitude two years in a row. The number of special awards is therefore going to be small—probably no more than 10 percent of the regular awards in any one year.

The advantage of special awards is that they help to blur, even if only a little, the arbitrary line of demarcation between regular eligibility and noneligibility. People who are not eligible understand that all hope is not lost and that magnificent performance will not go unrewarded.

There is a danger in special awards, however, and that is that the tail may wag the dog. At one huge company, the typical practice was to give 1,800 special awards each year, yet the regular eligibility list totaled only 1,000. When asked what percentage received special awards in two successive years, the personnel executive replied, "Oh, about 95 percent." Obviously, there was no longer anything special about that company's special awards.

Special awards, like regular awards, must be meaningful if they are truly to motivate. At the same company, the average special award was 3 percent of salary. When asked if awards of this level really motivated anybody, the personnel executive replied, "They're certainly not motivational, but we'd get one hell of a lot of demotivation if we cut them out!" His point illustrates the fact that companies can, if they are not careful, fall into a compensation trap from which it is very difficult to get free.

Award Levels

Awards should be both meaningful in size and at least competitive with the practices of other companies. They should also vary according to the position level. Table 1, shown earlier, indicates that the *average* bonus award as a percentage of salary in a diversified group of manufacturers ranges from 15 percent at the $30,000 base salary level to 50 percent at the $200,000 base salary level. There are two reasons to support the validity of this trend, one more pragmatic than the other.

First, the higher the position, the more visible the accomplishments or failures of the incumbent. And the more conspicuous the incumbent, the more risk he takes, for mediocrity of performance at high levels will not be tolerated for long. As noted earlier, a high degree of risk must·carry a high degree of reward.

Second, the higher the position, the higher the incumbent's base salary. And the higher the base salary, the higher the marginal income tax rate for additional ordinary income. Therefore, unless those in higher positions receive a greater percentage of pretax reward, their after-tax yield as a percentage of their after-tax salary will be less than that of others in lower-level positions.

These bonus ranges of 15 to 50 percent are, as noted, merely averages. Since any average is made up of a series of numbers, some higher and some lower, it follows that maximum bonus opportunities must be even greater than 15 to 50 percent. A maximum guideline of 130 percent of the average was used earlier in designing the integrated total compensation structure; applying this guideline to the 15 to 50 percent average produces potential maximum awards in the range of 50 to 95 percent of base salary ($30,000 base + 15 percent average bonus = $34,500 × 130 percent = $44,850 or 150 percent of base; $200,000 base + 50 percent average bonus = $300,000 × 130 percent = $390,000 or 195 percent of base).

Using the Integrated Compensation Ranges

We have been discussing bonus awards as percentages of base salary in order to illustrate certain trends, but such awards should really be administered in dollar terms within the integrated compensation structure to avoid possible pyramiding of compensation and the creation of other inequities.

Consider these two instances. First, we have an executive whose performance is outstanding but whose salary of $32,000 is 20 percent below the going rate. Our hypothetical company, employing the bonus trend line shown in Table 1, has adopted a policy calling for a 21 percent bonus for average performance and a 57 percent bonus for outstanding performance. Thus the executive receives a bonus of

$18,200 (57 percent of $32,000) and total compensation of $50,200. The problem in this case is that the 57 percent competitive bonus for outstanding performance was predicated on a salary equal to the going rate of $40,000; by rights, the executive should therefore have received total compensation of $62,900, which at his current salary rate of $32,000, would have required a 97 percent bonus.

Second, we have another executive in the same type of job as the first executive. His salary of $48,000 is 20 percent above the competitive rate but his performance is only average. Under the company's policy, he will receive a 21 percent bonus, giving him total compensation of $58,100. By rights, his bonus should have been predicated on the going rate and not on his actual salary. Applying a 21 percent bonus to a $40,000 salary produces total compensation of $48,400. Thus the bonus in this case should have been only $400—or, more likely, zero.

By using a percentage-of-base-salary approach to bonus determination, therefore, a company does very little to correct the inequities it currently has in its salary payments. And even when the compensation gap principle is used in salary determination, as discussed in Chapter 3, there are still going to be some salary inequities somewhere.

Thus award levels should be established not as a percentage of salary but as the dollar distance between the individual's current base salary and the targeted position in the total compensation range that has been established for his performance level. Such an approach corrects rather than perpetuates compensation inequities.

Of course, one concomitant of this approach is that the dollar amount of bonus paid to an individual whose salary is below his targeted range point will decrease as his salary approaches its correct level, unless he is simultaneously improving his performance. This pattern is considered to be demotivating by some executives. But again it comes down to a matter of choice. It seems far better to pay a man what he is worth when he is worth it than to keep him underpaid and create the illusion of steady growth. An executive searcher will tell it like it is the next time the phone rings—and there goes the illusion.

Determining What to "Incent"

Companies are in business to make profits, and so an annual executive bonus plan should presumably be designed to maximize the company's annual profits. That is almost invariably the case, but it is not enough to say that we are providing an incentive to maximize profits; we must define what we mean by profits.

Extraordinary items

Let's start with the bottom line on a company's income statement, the line that reads, "Net income after extraordinary items." Right away we have to decide whether the company's executives should be rewarded or penalized for achieving extraordinary gains or losses. And right away we have to align ourselves with one of two warring philosophical camps.

The first camp may be epitomized by the ancient precept that those who live by the sword must die by the sword. More recently, Harry Truman gave the precept contemporary significance by keeping a sign on his desk that read, "The buck stops here!" This camp believes in putting all the blame on management for anything that goes wrong, but it believes management should get all the credit too. Thus proponents of this reasoning would grab the bottom line on a company's income statement and hold to it fiercely.

The second camp, having been formed more recently, has no ancient precept. Its battle cry is less resounding than that of the first camp: People should be rewarded or penalized only for results under their control. On that basis, the people in this camp would exclude both extraordinary gains and extraordinary losses in defining profits.

As it turns out, the distance between the two camps is not all that great—at least as far as the issue of extraordinary items is concerned. That is because the Financial Accounting Standards Board, the rule-making body for the accounting profession, has recently issued a regulation that will severely limit the variety of transactions that can legitimately be reported as extraordinary items. In effect, FASB has itself adopted a philosophical stance which veers toward the live-by-the-sword camp.

As a compromise, some companies will define profits for bonus purposes as net income before extraordinary items, unless the board of directors or its compensation committee elects to include such items on a case-by-case basis. This approach is oriented more toward the control-over-results camp, since it implies that management should not be held accountable for any extraordinary item unless it can be truly blamed or credited for the item. Of course, this approach also throws the problem into the lap of the board, and if the board doesn't have enough detailed information to judge the events surrounding a particular extraordinary item, as is frequently the case, chances are that no extraordinary items will ever be included in the definition of profits for bonus plan purposes.

Income Taxes

Having resolved the issue of extraordinary items in one fashion or another, we come to the next line up from the bottom on the income statement, the one labeled "Net income after provision for income taxes." And once again we are plunged in controversy. Should the definition of profits for bonus plan purposes include or exclude income taxes?

The live-by-the-sword camp naturally remains glued to the bottom line. Their argument: Stockholders take their dividends and reinvested earnings out of after-tax profits. Why shouldn't executives do the same? If taxes go up and dividends have to be cut, why should executives get off scot-free?

The control-over-results camp looks at the matter differently. Executives cannot control the income tax rates levied on the corporation, so they should not be penalized or rewarded when tax rates change.

In recent years, the control-over-results camp seems to have taken its lumps over this particular argument. First, Congress has passed and then increased an investment tax credit. The amount of capital expenditures, and hence the amount of the credit itself, is certainly under the control of top management.

Second, there is a growing awareness that top executives are daily presented with many uncontrollables, tax rates simply being one of the more visible ones. Suppose you are a grocery retailer and your current supplier of shopping bags raises the price 10 percent. Naturally, you try to find another supplier whose price is lower. But suppose you can't. Do you stop supplying bags to your customers and leave them to balance 20 tin cans, 5 pounds of assorted meats, a dozen oranges, and 10 packages of frozen food in their arms? Inevitably, you end up paying the higher price for shopping bags, and then you try to find some other way to deliver the same bottom line profit. So you raise your prices a bit, if the market will stand for it, or you try to shave costs somewhere else. Wouldn't you try the same maneuvers if your tax rates went up? And if you would, how is an increase in tax rates different from an increase in the price of shopping bags, except perhaps in degree?

Because of these factors, the balance appears to be tilting toward the live-by-the-sword camp. In years past the majority of executive bonus plans were predicated on pretax profits, but today the majority of new plans seem to be based on aftertax profits.

For the sake of argument, however, let's suppose a company has decided to use pretax profits as the basis for its executive bonus plan. The company then begins to look at the costs that go into the determination of pretax profits, and it discovers a charge for the cost of the bonus plan itself. Is that a problem? Consider this dialogue between the CEO of a small company and his controller.

> CONTROLLER: Well, boss, it looks as though the pretax profits will be coming in at just about $1 million this year.
> CEO: That's great. Since our executive team gets 20 percent of the pretax profits, we'll have a bonus fund of $200,000. Right?
> CONTROLLER: Well, not exactly. If we pay bonuses of $200,000 that will drop the pretax profits to $800,000 and we'd be exceeding the 20-percent-of-profits bonus limit.
> CEO: Oh, I see what you mean. So the bonus fund will be only $160,000, or 20 percent of the $800,000, right?
> CONTROLLER: Well, not exactly. If we pay bonuses of $160,000, that will drop the pretax profits to $840,000, and in that case we'd be cheating ourselves out of the full 20-percent-of-profits fund.

Thus leaving the accrued charges for bonuses in the definition of pretax profits causes a company to have to chase its own tail, so to speak. Because of this, most companies define profits as being before any charges for bonuses are levied against profits. If they are using pretax profits as the basis for the bonus plan, they add back to pretax profits any amounts already accrued against profits for bonuses. And if they are using aftertax profits as the basis of the plan, they add back to such profits an amount equal to the aftertax cost of the bonus accrual. For example, consider the company that is at a 48 percent marginal tax rate and has already charged $1 million against pretax profits for executive bonuses. Its add-back to aftertax profits would be $520,000, since that is the amount by which aftertax profits would be depressed were the charges not reversed out of income.

Of course, the conventional wisdom may not always be applicable. Consider this actual case:

A company's executives were collectively promised a bonus fund of $150,000 if pretax profits were $1 million or more. By December it looked as though the profits would peak out at $970,000 for the year. So the executives got together a kitty of $35,000 ($5,000 extra just to be on the safe side), dummied up a sales order, and contributed the money to the company's revenues. Since there were no costs for this sale, the entire $35,000 dropped down to pretax profits. The result? Final pretax profits exceeded $1 million and the executives received their $150,000 fund.

In the trade, such a plan design is said to have a go, no-go feature or, as it is sometimes called, a cliff effect. No funds are created up to a specified point in the profit stream, then a large fund is created if profits advance by only a single dollar. Obviously, such a design should be resisted because there is an invitation to fraud at the go, no-go point. Certainly, the company's stockholders, an otherwise greedy lot, would not want to see that last extra dollar of profit generated if it would cost them $150,000. However, such a feature is sometimes necessary for other reasons, and if it is, the impact can at least be mitigated by defining profits as being *after* the costs of the bonus plan itself have been charged to profits. This would allow executives to receive 100 percent of the incremental profits for a time, but only for a time. And there would never be any point in the profit stream where they would stand to receive more than the incremental profits.

Divisional Bonus Plans

Let us move back to the income statement. Suppose our hypothetical company was planning to develop a new bonus plan for a particular division rather than for the company as a whole. Further, suppose the company had already decided to predicate bonuses on divisional profits before income taxes and before the costs of the new bonus plan have been charged to profits. A further open issue remains, and that concerns the inclusion or exclusion of allocated charges for corporate overhead. The live-by-the-sword camp says the division should be made to take its fair share of corporate overhead charges, because such charges are simply another cost of doing business. What is more, the division is receiving services which it would otherwise have to buy directly.

The control-over-results camp rejoins that corporate overhead is a classic case of an uncontrollable charge and hence should be excluded when figuring divisional profits for bonus purposes.

In general, the CEO of the parent company will want to charge out his corporate overhead. One CEO had this to say about keeping his corporate overhead under control. "It's difficult for me to assess the merit of the finance department's claim that it needs two more budget analysts. When I charge out all my overhead to the divisions, I get endless complaints from the division general managers, and their complaints give me a chance to keep my corporate departments in line. Besides, if I didn't charge out overhead, the division general managers would want to transfer a lot of their people over to the corporate staff and have us hire a few more to boot. After all, what do they care if they don't have to pay the bill?"

In general, division management executives take just the opposite tack, and for obvious reasons.

Should divisions be charged for corporate overhead when designing a divisional bonus plan? Perhaps the problem can be summed up by the following conversation, which took place during the visit of a Chicago-based division general manager to his company's New York headquarters:

> CEO: Hi, Joe. What are you doing in town today?
>
> DGM: Just here for a budget planning meeting. I thought I'd stick my head in the door and say hello. In fact, while I'm at it, I have a bone to pick with you. You know, you give me hard enough profit targets as it is, but then every month I get a long computer printout showing the overhead charges you're incurring in this puzzle palace you're running here in New York. It's damn hard for me to deliver the profits I'm responsible for, but with those overhead charges you're throwing at me, it's well-nigh impossible.
>
> CEO: Listen, Joe, you ought to consider yourself lucky you're not getting all the service you're paying for.

After he thought about the matter for a bit, the division general manager had to concede the validity of his CEO's point.

We've now gone through the various definitions of profits that can be used for executive bonus plan purposes, but we're still not entirely through the process of answering the question: What do we want to incent?

The Importance of Return on Investment

An incentive for profits, no matter how the term is ultimately defined, says little or nothing about an incentive for conservation of capital.

For example, if I have an incentive for pretax profits alone, I could sell another $100 million of stock to the public and, for want of any better alternative, invest the extra money in certificates of deposit at 7 percent interest. Such a strategy would increase my pretax profits by $7 million dollars a year. I'd be happy because the extra pretax profits would give me a larger bonus. But would the stockholders be happy with the return I was earning on their incremental investment?

So the incentive plan designer has to confront the additional question: How important is return on investment to the business? Certainly, there *are* cases where ROI is not important, but such cases are rare. For example, one of New York's advertising agency executives was heard to say, "95 percent of my inventory goes down in the elevator every night." In his case, the need for capital was negligible— some office space (leased) and some desks and chairs. But how about the oil company that drops $500 million into a single refinery project?

Earnings per Share

There are four ways to measure a company's return on investment for executive bonus plan purposes. The first is earnings per share. Here profits, however defined, are divided by the number of shares outstanding. Using earnings per share offers a capital conservation of sorts, but it is a relatively mild one. If the company needs more capital, it can cut its dividend (either absolutely or relative to the increasing earnings) and divert more aftertax profits to retained earnings. This does not trigger an increase in the number of shares outstanding. What is more, the incremental retained earnings come interest-free, and hence any return on such earnings goes right into profits and further increases the earnings per share.

If that strategy still won't raise enough capital, the company can try to borrow the funds required. Here interest will have to be paid, but any incremental return on the debt that exceeds the interest payment will also flow through to profits and hence to earnings per share. In this case as well, the total number of shares outstanding remains constant. So, the only time that an earnings per share incentive has ROI teeth in it vis-à-vis a straight profit incentive is when the company cannot raise enough capital from both retained earnings and debt sources and thus has to sell more shares on the open market.

Another criticism that is sometimes leveled at the earnings per share measure is that it may give top executives an incentive to leverage the company, taking on additional debt when they should be selling more equity and thereby exposing the company to a disaster in the event that profits dip substantially and render if difficult or impossible to service the higher debt load. On the other hand, it can be argued that the board of directors has to approve major capital decisions. Presumably, the board would not allow the company to become overleveraged with debt (a presumption that has gone down in flames more than a few times.)

Return on Stockholders' Equity

The second way of measuring ROI is to use return on stockholders' equity. The numerator of this fraction is profits, however defined. The denominator consists of the sum of (1) capital stock, (2) capital surplus, and (3) retained earnings (or earned surplus, as it is sometimes called), measured either as of the beginning of the fiscal year or as the average during the year.

This measure of return on investment has more teeth in it than earnings per share because executives are required to earn a decent return, not just on the monies received from the sale of new shares but also on the monies received through retention of earnings that are not paid out in dividends. On the other hand, an incentive to leverage the company still exists.

Return on Capital Employed

The third way of measuring ROI is to use return on capital employed. Here the numerator is the sum of (1) profits, however defined, and (2) amounts charged against profits, however defined, for interest on long-term debt having a maturity of more than one year. The denominator of the fraction consists of the sum of (1) stockholders' equity and (2) long-term debt having a maturity of more than one year.

Capital employed—equity plus long-term debt—represents the permanent capital any company has to work with, and some analysts believe that it is the best measure of return on investment. Among other things, the potential incentive to leverage the company with debt disappears when using return on capital employed, since management is charged with producing an adequate return on *all* permanent capital in the business, not just equity capital.

When using this measure, however, it is necessary, as is shown above, to reverse out of profits any interest costs on the long-term debt included in the investment base. Otherwise, management ends up, not with an incentive to leverage the company, but with an unintended incentive to go too far in eliminating debt. That is because there would be a double-barreled penalty for taking on additional debt (reduction in profits because of interest charges plus increase in the investment base due to the greater debt) as compared to only a single-barreled penalty for taking on additional equity (no reduction in profits because no interest charges are incurred, but an increase in the investment base due to the greater equity). By reversing out interest charges from profits, management receives the same single penalty for taking on either additional equity or additional long-term debt.

Return on Assets

The fourth and final commonly used measure of ROI is return on assets. Here the numerator of the equation is the sum of (1) profits, however defined, and (2) amounts charged against profits, however defined, for interest on *all* debt, whether short term or long term. The denominator is total assets.

Since total assets equal total liabilities (at least in the more soundly run companies), the difference between using assets and using capital employed as the investment base lies in the amounts included under current liabilities. By using return on assets as its measure of ROI, a company is charging its executives with earning a suitable return on *all* capital in the business, including even temporary short-term borrowings needed for such things as financing receivables and inventories.

Use of ROI Measures

To what extent are these four measures of ROI used? Few companies use earnings per share in an annual executive bonus plan, because shares outstanding—the denominator of the fraction—may increase not at all or hardly at all in a single year, or it may increase by a huge jump as the company makes a major equity offering or issues large amounts of stock to acquire another company. In the first instance there is no real incentive to conserve capital; in the second, the huge jump could cause bonuses to plummet without good cause, if the new capital created by the share issuance cannot be deployed immediately. On the other hand, quite a few companies use earnings per share as their measure of performance for long-term incentive compensation. More on this later.

For different reasons, few companies use return on assets except when designing divisional bonus plans. The argument here seems to be that return on assets is a needlessly stringent measure of ROI that could be distorted by short-term swings in inventories and accounts receivable.

That leaves the great bulk of companies using either return on stockholders' equity or return on capital employed as incentive measures for their executive bonus plans. Probably, slightly more companies use return on stockholders' equity. But fashions change with the economic environment. When the economy is booming and there seems to be no tomorrow, companies tend to favor return on stockholders' equity because that measure allows them to do some creative leveraging. But when times are bad, attention turns to a clean balance sheet with little or no debt. It is during these times that return on capital employed seems to be the measure of preference. Among very capital-intensive companies it is also possible to discern a pattern—though not a sharply pronounced one—of popularity for return on capital employed. It is these companies that worry most about earning a decent return on the prodigious amounts of capital they consume.

The Deductible

Having threaded through the maze of possibilities posed by the question: "What do I want to incent?" the incentive plan designer must next decide at what point in the profit stream he wishes to generate bonus funds.

When times were simpler it used to be common practice to adopt a bonus funding formula that said it all in one sentence: Executives will receive 3 percent of pretax profits. But as base salaries and fringe benefits rose, a pertinent question came to be raised: If executives get a slice of even the first dollar of profit, why are we paying them base salaries? They ought to be required to earn their keep before they get extra bonus money.

The point was well taken, and companies began to revise their bonus funding formulas accordingly. For example, one company that had been granting executives bonuses equal to 3 percent of pretax profits restated its formula to provide 6 percent of all pretax profits in excess of $50 million.

This approach had some merit, but it also had an obvious tendency to become outdated by events. The company had established this $50 million "deductible" at a time when it was earning $100 million in pretax profits. Today the company's pretax profits are in excess of $300 million; obviously the $50 million deductible no longer has the teeth it once had.

Because of this, and because, over time, companies began to stress the need for a decent ROI, not merely decent raw profits, it became natural to define the deductible in terms of the ROI measure. A company would tell its executives that no funds for bonuses would be generated until the return on stockholders' equity (or return on capital employed) reached x percent, the fund consisting of y percent of any additional profits. With the deductible not a fixed but a floating number, the dollar amount of the deductible increased as the investment base increased.

But what percentage return should the deductible represent? Obviously, the higher the percentage return selected as the deductible, the higher the funding leverage. Once the funding threshold has been passed, when profits are going up the operation of any deductible causes the executive bonus fund to increase at a rate faster than the increase in profits, and when profits are going down the operation of the deductible causes the fund to decrease faster than the decrease in profits. And the higher the deductible, the more bonus swing or leverage will be built into the plan.

Alternative Economic Benefit

Companies tend to take one of three philosophical stances in selecting the percentage return they will employ as a deductible. The first and most minimal stance rests on the theory of alternative economic benefit. The argument goes something like this: The stockholders could invest their money in a savings account, in government bonds, or in some other risk-free medium and could earn 7 percent, more or less, on such an investment (depending on what is happening with interest rates). If we can't earn at least that return on their money, what with the risks they are taking, we shouldn't be in business. At the least, we shouldn't be paying anyone a bonus. Using this line of argument, a company might establish a deductible equal to a 7 percent aftertax return on stockholders' equity. If the company were employing a plan based on pretax profits, the required return might be 14 percent, given a marginal tax rate of 50 percent (to use a round number). With a plan based on return on capital employed, the company would probably select a percentage return that would generate sufficient profits after taxes and after interest costs to represent a 7 percent return on stockholders' equity.

Returns of Comparable Companies

The second philosophical stance in selecting a percentage return figure is posited on the actual returns achieved by a panel of comparable companies. The company might select 20 or so companies in its industry and then pick a percentage return equal to, say, the 10th or 25th percentile of the distribution. In other words, the percentage return selected would be minimal in relation to the actual performance of the companies being studied, but it would also be at least equal to, and probably higher than, the percentage return derived through the first philosophical stance.

The third philosophical stance is predicated on the company's own history. The reasoning might go something like this: Stockholders ought to be able to earn at least 7 percent on their investment. But that's not nearly enough. Look at our own industry, where the company with the poorest performance is clearing a 10 percent return on its stockholder equity. But even that figure leaves much to be desired. In the past ten years our company has never earned less than a 14 percent aftertax return on stockholders' equity, and our average has been 17 percent. Therefore, I can't see how our deductible can be anything less than a 14 percent return on stockholders' equity, or maybe a 13 percent return if you hit me on a generous day.

Most companies implicitly adopt the first philosophical stance. It is, after all, not unreasonable on its face, nor is it too gutsy. With the second philosophical stance there is no guarantee that the number chosen will not quickly become invalid. Suppose that the low-performing companies on the competitor panel start improving their returns. Or suppose our hypothetical company enters another industry to such an extent that its competitor panel is no longer appropriate. The third philosophical stance locks the company into its own high-performance history. If the company is willing to pay superlative bonuses for clearing its very high deductible, that's one thing. But if it isn't, the result is likely to be payment of average bonuses for outstanding performance.

The Bonus Funding Formula

At this point let us assume that the incentive plan designer has selected aftertax return on stockholders' equity as the incentive measure for the new executive bonus plan and has further decided that the plan should employ a deductible equal to 7 percent of stockholders' equity. He now has to decide what portion of profits above the deductible should be diverted to the eligible executives.

In arriving at his decision, let us assume that he has the following facts in his possession:

- Stockholders' equity is expected to average $500 million during the next year.
- Aggregate norm bonuses payable for average performance are $1 million. This figure is derived by subtracting the sum of actual base salaries for all bonus eligibles from the sum of total cash compensation control points for all eligibles.
- Average performance among comparable companies consists of a 10 percent return on stockholders' equity.

Given these facts, the designer will probably develop the following funding formula: 6.67 percent of aftertax profits in excess of a 7 percent return on stockholders' equity.

To test this formula, assume first that the company achieves an average 10 percent return on stockholders' equity. Since the stockholders' equity is expected to be $500 million, a 10 percent return will yield aftertax profits of $50 million. However, the first $35 million of profits doesn't count, since that amount represents the deductible of 7 percent on stockholders' equity. Accordingly, the corridor of profits from which funds for bonuses will be drawn is $15 million, consisting of the difference between actual profits of $50 million and the deductible of $35 million. If 6.67 percent of this $15 million corridor is diverted to executive bonuses, the fund so produced will equal the $1 million needed to pay the required norm bonuses for average performance.

In practice the designer would probably round up the multiplier (the term used for the percentage of profits above the deductible that is being diverted to the executives) to an even 7 percent, since an odd multiplier like 6.67 percent probably raises more questions than it answers. And besides, a little extra funding capacity isn't a bad thing to have.

Sideline Limitations

While he was at it, the designer might also decide to impose certain sideline limitations on the bonus fund. For example, in addition to adopting the above formula he might specify that no funds be payable unless (1) the company declared a dividend, or (2) the company's dividends per share were not less than $1.50, or (3) the company's earnings per share were not less than $4, and so on. In general, such sideline limitations are purely cosmetic. They are incorporated to reassure the stockholders that management is looking out for their interests, but the limitations imposed are usually so loose that nothing less than a disaster would wipe out the bonus fund. And in that event you can be sure the company would have a different plan designer the next time around.

In somewhat different circumstances, the plan designer might have a real problem on his hands. Suppose, for example, that the company insisted on a deductible equal to a 9 percent return on stockholders' equity instead of a minimal 7 percent return. In that case, the designer would have to use a multiplier of 20 percent of profits above the deductible to generate a $1 million bonus fund at the point of average performance. (Average performance equals a 10 percent return equals $50 million less $45 million deductible equals a $5 million corridor times 20 percent equals $1 million in bonus funds.) If he did use such a multiplier, he would face two further problems.

First, the company's stockholders might scream. They could charge, and rightfully so, that few if any comparable companies were using such a high multiplier. Of course, they would be overlooking the fact that few if any comparable companies were using such a high deductible either.

Second, the fund would swing wildly with any changes in profitability. If actual profits were $47.5 million instead of $50 million, the fund would be cut in half. And if actual profits were $60 million instead of $50 million, the fund would triple to $3 million—or three times the amount needed to pay norm bonuses. Clearly, more funds would be required for such outstanding performance. But not that much more.

In this sort of situation, the plan designer might be well advised to eliminate the deductible altogether and move to a formula such as this: No bonus funds will be created unless profits after taxes and *after* the costs of bonuses are equal to or greater than 9 percent of stockholders' equity. Thereafter, the bonus fund will consist of 2 percent of *all* such profits.

Note the changes in this approach. First, the deductible has been eliminated, and there will be no bonus if return on stockholders' equity dips below 9 percent. Second, the definition of profits has been revised to include charges for the plan itself. This change assures that the creation of bonus funds will not of itself cause return on stockholders' equity to drop below 9 percent. Third, the multiplier is much smaller—2 percent as against 20 percent. And fourth, the swing in the plan has been reduced substantially (perhaps too substantially) because the multiplier is smaller.

Turning the Faucet On

To see how this plan works, envisage the profits as flowing through two faucets, one labeled "Stockholders" and the second labeled "Executives." As profits begin to be generated, only the stockholder faucet is turned on. This continues to be the case until $45 million in profits are produced—an amount equal to a 9 percent return on stockholders' equity. At this point the stockholder faucet is turned off and the executive faucet is turned on. All additional profits flow through the executive faucet until the total reaches $900,000—or 2 percent of $45 million. Then the executive faucet is turned down to a 2 percent flow rate, the stockholder faucet is turned on to a 98 percent flow rate, and both faucets continue to flow as further profits are produced. Accordingly, as profits rise to $50 million, an extra $100,000 flows through the executive faucet, thus achieving the desired $1 million fund. (For the sake of simplicity we have ignored the fact that after-tax bonus accruals depress profits and hence slightly lower the fund.)

Stockholder Approval

There is no federal law mandating stockholder approval for an executive bonus plan. However, such plans may require stockholder approval if the company is incorporated in certain states. Additionally, if the plan is to involve payments in company stock and if the company is listed on the New York Stock Exchange, that exchange has rules mandating stockholder approval of proposed plans.

The fact is that most companies seek stockholder approval anyway. Stockholder approval is seen to have good public relations value, and it may have legal value as well. In a number of states the burden of proof that excessive bonuses have been paid shifts from the company to the suing stockholder where stockholder approval had previously been obtained.

Typically the plan submitted to the stockholders for approval is a facade behind which the real plan lurks. It consists of these elements:

- The purpose of the plan—typically a "salute the flag" statement.
- A statement of eligibility for awards—generally some bland reference to key employees.
- A statement of administration of the plan—generally vested in a committee of disinterested directors.
- The funding formula.
- A statement that the funding formula cannot be increased without prior stockholder approval.
- The payment methods and form, such as cash in a lump sum, or a choice of cash or stock, or deferrals.

This is not to suggest that the plan as approved by the stockholders is purely a cosmetic exercise. When all is said and done, the funding formula assures stockholders that management may spend less on bonuses but never more than the agreed-upon amount. And presumably, the formula is also reasonable on its face, demonstrating to stockholders that they are getting the lion's share of any profits the company makes.

The Allocation Process

To see how the incentive plan works in practice, we have to look behind the official text. In a small company, bonus awards for individual executives can be determined as soon as the size of the overall fund is known. But this is not practical in a company with, say 500 eligible executives. Because of this, larger companies utilize various methods to whack the overall fund into appropriate pieces for various organizational units. If the company is large enough, each piece may also be whacked into smaller pieces before the process of determining the award for a single individual begins.

Subjective Allocation

The earliest allocation process—and one still used widely today—involves subjective judgments made at the end of the year. First, the CEO has to decide whether to spend all the funds produced by the funding formula that year (or to spend all the funds and then some by dipping into reserves from earlier years). When a bonus funding formula is new, there is a tendency to spend almost all the funds because the formula is custom-tailored to the company's bonus-spending needs. However, if the company has been successful the formula may in time generate too large a fund. This is because increases in the fund typically are disproportionate to increases in profits, yet the number of eligibles added to the plan typically increases at a slower rate than the profits. Then, too, the eligibles being added generally receive relatively lower norm bonuses since they are at the bottom of the eligibility spectrum.

To illustrate, let us assume that the CEO needs $1 million to pay each eligible his norm bonus and $2 million to pay each eligible his maximum bonus. The fund is $2.5 million. At the same time the CEO subjectively decides that company performance that year was above average but not uniformly outstanding. On that basis he decides that an overall expenditure of $1.5 million would be appropriate. He now has to subdivide this $1.5 million fund among his profit centers and corporate departments.

First the CEO turns his gaze on Profit Center A, taking into account how that unit performed against its profit budget and any other major goals it may have been assigned to accomplish during the past year. He concludes that Profit Center A has performed about as well as the company generally (which means above average compared to the outside world). Given the decision to allocate $1.5 million in bonus funds instead of an average distribution of $1 million, the CEO allocates this unit an amount halfway between that required to pay each eligible in the unit a norm bonus and that required to pay each eligible a maximum bonus.

Then the CEO looks at Profit Center B. In this case he concludes that an outstanding job was done, and he gives Profit Center B an allocation amount three-quarters of the way between that unit's aggregate norm bonus and aggregate maximum bonus needs.

The CEO doesn't like what he sees when he looks at Profit Center C. Not only has this unit not performed relatively as well as the other units in the company, but it has performed below average compared to the outside world. So the CEO gives this unit an amount equal only to 75 percent of that required to pay each eligible a norm bonus.

After he has taken a first cut at allocating the fund, the CEO adds up the various numbers. If they total less than $1.5 million, he may well let them stand unchanged, or he may increase each unit's allocation ratably until the $1.5 million fund is exhausted. If the allocations total more than $1.5 million, he may decrease each unit's allocation ratably. Or, if he is feeling particularly generous, he may let the figures stand unchanged, rationalizing that perhaps he had underestimated the company's performance. After all, there's still plenty of money left.

Deficiencies of Subjective Allocation

This allocation approach has the single virtue of being highly flexible. Within the limits imposed by the funding formula, the CEO can do anything he wants. It also has numerous deficiencies, the first of which is that it is shrouded in mystery. The overall fund produced by the formula is like a pie whose diameter is proportional to the size of the fund. The pie is wheeled into the CEO's office at the end of the year, and taking up a broadsword, he hacks it into a number of pieces. For this task he needs a steady hand, because an extra segment could represent $100,000 of funding.

The CEO then calls in the group heads who supervise multiple profit centers and gives each a piece. Each group head now retires to his own office and wields his own ax to divide the piece into several smaller pieces, one for each profit center.

The profit center head then cuts his piece into yet smaller pieces for each department head within the profit center. Finally, the head of marketing, say, slices off minuscule pieces for various marketing executives. At the end of this elaborate process, the individual executive receives a sliver of the pie. He has no idea why he got what he got and no idea as to how he can get more next year.

Compare this process with our way of dealing with our own children. On a Saturday afternoon you call Junior and tell him to mow the lawn. Having quietly observed your behavior over the years, he asks: "How much are you going to pay me?" You reply: "Do a good job and I'll see." What you see, about a half hour later, is Junior mowing the neighbor's lawn for $5, contracted for in advance. And he's using your mower and gas to boot!

Perhaps executives of yesteryear were content with the do-a-good-job-and-we'll-see philosophy. But that is not the case any longer.

Another problem with the allocation approach just described is that the degree of discretion utilized in a discretionary bonus plan seemingly is inversely correlated with the degree of discretion that can be utilized. If the CEO can do anything he wants with the bonus fund, he will probably do nothing, giving each unit the same relative allocation. In more than a few companies the CEO is reminiscent of the Wizard of Oz. Behind the smoke, fire, and fearsome noises is an ordinary mortal who wants everyone to love him and who gets upset when they don't. This kind of CEO is happy to give one unit a lot extra until he finds that he is playing a zero sum game and must therefore give some other unit a lot less. It is at this point that his ability to rationalize comes into play. "So the new product introduction was a flop. So payroll costs got out of line. So the division fell below budget. Well, no one's perfect. And besides, they're all trying to do the right thing." In the end the mediocre unit gets a full allocation, and the outstanding unit gets nothing extra to recognize its outstanding performance.

This is not to imply that a company should never use discretionary allocation. Perhaps there is no better alternative. Moreover, the process can be improved upon if every eligible is given enough information on which to judge its fairness. For example, the CEO may be compelled to tell a profit center head, "You are getting a fund equal to 150 percent of your norm awards, other profit centers are getting between 50 percent and 175 percent of their norm awards, and the average profit center is getting 125 percent of its norm awards." The profit center head then has enough information to assess whether the CEO is playing fair. And there is a greater probability that the CEO will monitor his own behavior and really play fair.

Allocation Tied to Goals

A different allocation process involves the establishment of specific goals at the beginning of the year and the linkage of known amounts of money to the accomplishment of those goals. Instead of saying to the profit center head, "Do a good job and I'll see," the CEO tells him, "If your pretax profits are less than $30 million, you will get no fund at all. If your pretax profits are $35 million, you will receive a fund equal to aggregate norm bonuses. If your pretax profits are $40 million or more, you will receive a fund equal to aggregate maximum bonuses. Interpolation will be used for intermediate profit points."

In this case the CEO is acting more like the next-door neighbor who is wise enough to know that the best way to motivate desired behavior is to spell out in advance the conditions that will obtain if the behavior is forthcoming.

Of course, this approach is not as simple as it appears to be at first glance. For example, one CEO told his division heads: "Our corporate goal this year is to increase profits by at least 10 percent. Any division that increases its profits by that amount gets a fund equal to its aggregate norm bonuses, and any division that increases its profits 15 percent gets a fund equal to its aggregate maximum bonuses."

The problem here was that each division had a different capacity for growth in that year. One division had a hot new product line and customers breaking down the doors; it could have achieved a 15 percent profit increase if all the executives had stayed in bed until it was time to collect their bonuses. Another division was spending millions on research and development, was operating at a huge loss, and had every expectation that the loss would widen before it began to shrink. Thus a fixed growth goal may have been reasonable for the corporation as a whole, but it was patently unreasonable for individual profit centers.

In a way, today's modern diversified corporation is not unlike a hospital. Some patients are well and require little care. But there is also a nursery where premature babies are struggling to make it with the help of incubators. And there is an intensive care unit where old people are struggling to make it with the aid of cardiac monitors and respirators. Obviously, the same treatment cannot be extended to every patient.

Because of this, the company that wants to set goals in advance for each profit center and then link bonus funds to these goals in a predetermined fashion has to be able to set so-called *equal stretch* goals. The CEO has to be able to say to his division managers: "Our corporate goal this year is to increase profits by at least 10 percent. In order for us to make this goal, I'm going to need a 30 percent profit increase from Profit Center A, a 20 percent profit increase from Profit Center B, 10 percent increases from Profit Centers C and D, and no more than a $5 million loss from Profit Center E. In my opinion, each of these goals will require about the same amount of effort and good luck."

Allocation Tied to Budgets

Typically, companies employing this allocation approach rely on their profit budgeting mechanisms to get there. The division manager is told he will receive a fund equal to aggregate norm awards if his division exactly achieves its budget. He is also told how much he can sink below budget before the fund disappears and how much he has to grow above budget to get the maximum fund.

This is an acceptable approach—on paper. But its validity obviously depends on the validity of the budgetary process itself. And the most obvious of the many problems inherent in the budgetary process is the conflict of interest built into it. If I am a division manager and I know that bonus funds will be linked to my budget, isn't it likely that I will try for the lowest budget I can get away with? Probably. But some division managers, usually those who came up through marketing and are filled with optimism, will propose a wildly high budget that can be achieved only if absolutely everything goes right. These executives use the budget to exhort their troops to greater glory.

Then, too, the CEO himself may not be exactly neutral during budget setting. If he wants to give the board a lofty number and the summation of the proposed division budgets is low, he too may indulge in a bit of games playing. He may increase each division's budget proportionately, ignoring the fact that there may be differences in stretch among the various division proposals, or he may try to figure out which divisions are sandbagging him and give them the lion's share of the burden of extra profits he is demanding. In either case, he may be making a mistake.

Clearly, this second allocation approach has the potential to be motivationally better than the first, totally discretionary approach, but it is no panacea, and it may end in disaster if the company doesn't have a good budget-setting infrastructure.

Division Incentives

In following this approach, the question arises as to whether a division should be offered an incentive for raw profits or, like the company itself, for return on investment. Obviously, a division has no stockholders' equity or capital employed that can be easily isolated. In fact, most divisions have only the asset side of the balance sheet plus current liabilities. So if an ROI incentive is to be used, it will probably be return on assets. Often such an incentive is introduced by levying a capital charge against the division's profits for the use of all capital or capital beyond some predetermined point. The division head is told: Your profit budget is $40 million, and to make this budget we assume you will need average assets of $300 million. If your actual average assets exceed this amount, your profits will be debited by 8 percent of the excess. If your actual average assets are below this amount, your profits will be credited by 8 percent of the deficiency.

Other companies are content to give their divisions an incentive only for raw profits, even though the corporate funding formula is predicated on, say, return on stockholders' equity. They reason that they will control major increments to capital through a tight capital budgeting procedure, and they also reason that the particular profit budget imposed on the division contains an intrinsically acceptable return on investment. Of course, the division could get sloppy with inventories and receivables during the year, and these incremental assets might escape the attention of the capital control mechanisms.

But many CEO's believe they can spot such problems without overly complicating their bonus plans.

Companies employing this second allocation approach generally develop an additional corporate funding formula to generate bonuses for corporate executives on the same essential basis as the divisional funding formulas generate them for divisional executives. If a division is to receive aggregate norm bonuses for meeting its profit budget, a corporate staff department will receive aggregate norm bonuses for meeting the corporate profit budget.

This second corporate funding formula can be termed an internal funding formula, because it is not submitted to shareholders for approval, and is often revised annually to meet a particular year's profit objectives. However, the internal funding formula must operate within the confines of the stockholder-approved one, which, for purposes of discussion, can be called the external funding formula. Companies proceeding this way often have an external formula that produces more funding than they actually need. Rather than ask the shareholders to change the formula, they leave it in place, operate within newly created internal funding formulas, and cast the external funding formula in the role of a circuit breaker. Like its electrical analogue, its sole function is to trip in when an overload occurs and save the house from burning down.

This approach seems to make good sense, except where there is games playing in setting the corporate budget. Not uncommonly, all the hopes and dreams of the CEO are dumped on the divisions, and each is given a wild profit budget. When the various division budgets are brought together, however, the corporate budget, even before being adjusted for exclusively corporate expenses, is considerably lower than the summation of the division budgets. In effect, the CEO exhorts his troops to greater glory, but he himself would rather sit comfortably behind the front lines.

Once a company has developed its internal divisional and internal corporate funding formulas, it must then decide whether all or only a part of division bonuses should be predicated on division performance. For example, the CEO might tell a division manager: If your division achieves its budget you will receive a fund equal to your aggregate norm bonuses, and you will receive this fund under all conditions unless the corporation does so badly as to have insufficient funds under its stockholder-approved funding formula. If that funding formula has plenty of extra capacity, the division manager can be reasonably sure of getting his full funding even when the corporation as a whole is having a fairly poor year.

On the other hand, the CEO might tell the division manager: Half your funding will be riding on your division's results and the other half on corporate results. If your division meets its profit budget, you will receive a fund equal to half your aggregate norm bonuses. If the corporation meets its profit budget, you will receive a fund equal to half your aggregate norm bonuses. Each fund will operate independently. If your division exceeds its budget while the corporation undershoots its budget, you will receive more than half your aggregate norm bonuses from the division fund and less than half, or perhaps nothing, from the corporate fund. Of course, all funding is subject to the limits imposed by the stockholder-approved external funding formula.

What we are dealing with here is interdivisional teamwork. Obviously, if no division ever sells or buys products from a sister division, and if no division ever transfers people to or receives people from a sister division, and if each division utilizes a technology that is different from any other division, basing each division's bonus funds entirely on its own results may be entirely appropriate. But what if the divisions *do* sell to or buy from one another, *do* transfer people to or receive people from one another, and *do* utilize a common technology? In that case, some corporate teamwork incentive is obviously needed to keep the company from flying apart through sheer centrifugal force.

In the example used earlier, 50 percent of awards were funded through the internal division formula and 50 percent of the awards were funded through the internal corporate formula, but that does not have to be the case. Depending on the degree of interdivisional teamwork actually needed, the split might be 75:25 or 25:75, or any other combination that seems appropriate.

All along we have been referring to the stockholder-approved external funding formula and indicating that it might cut in at some point to reduce or even eliminate the bonuses earned by an outstanding division. Should this be the case?

Some companies with independently operating divisions have concluded that, to obtain maximum motivation, the divisions should be guaranteed bonus funds if they perform, even though the corporation as a whole is having a disaster. To do this, they separate the divisional bonus plans from the stockholder-approved bonus plans. The latter then applies only to the corporate staff departments and the CEO.

Critics of this approach maintain that the company's bonus levels will go out of control. But proponents argue that it is not necessary to have stockholder-approved controls over *every* bonus eligible. They believe such controls over just the CEO and a handful of other corporate executives will do the trick.

In a way, the typical CEO is like the queen in *Snow White*. Every night he faces his mirror and says: "Mirror, mirror, on the wall, who is the highest paid of all?" And if the mirror replies, "Not you," there's trouble in the company the next morning! If that reflects the truth, it may be sufficient to control only the CEO's compensation. He in turn will make quite sure that everyone else is paid "properly"—meaning substantially less than he is.

Besides, there is considerable merit in the remarks made by one CEO at an annual meeting, when a dissident stockholder challenged the payment of a large bonus to the head of a major division in a year when the corporation had lost $20 million. "I didn't get a bonus, and I didn't deserve one. And neither did my corporate department heads and all the other division managers. But this particular division considerably exceeded its very ambitious profit budget and turned in absolutely outstanding performance. If that hadn't occurred, the company would have lost $30 million instead of $20 million. I believe in paying for performance, and that division manager performed."

When External Events Impinge

We have seen that this second allocation process is preferable motivationally to the first, provided that the company is capable of setting truly equal-stretch goals for its various units. But even the most well-honed plans can go awry and be subverted by uncontrollable external events. For example, consider what happened to profit budget assumptions after OPEC quintupled the price of oil. Or consider what happened to profit budget assumptions in a candy company when the price of sugar suddenly went through the roof one year and just as suddenly dropped the next year. Or consider what happened to a company's international division when the Financial Accounting Standards Board decreed that the full effects of a major devaluation of a foreign currency had to be taken into income right away.

In all these cases and more, the profit budget was based on a set of rational assumptions. Then, during the year, an event of major proportions occurred—an event that was totally outside the control of management.

Once again, we have to listen to the live-by-the-sword camp and the control-over-results camp. The former says: "So what! Bad things happen, but good things happen, too, and you never hear about them. It's the case of the old Chinese proverb, victory has a thousand fathers and defeat none." The control-over-results camp is equally adamant, of course: "How can you penalize a division manager because some guy wearing a white sheet quintupled the price of oil, or because some bean counter in the Financial Accounting Standards Board had a brainstorm?"

In a way, both arguments have right on their side. Obviously, you can't pay a division manager a huge bonus for dropping 80 percent below his profit budget, just because the reason for the decline was out of his control. The stockholders have to take their lumps, after all, and no one is going to bail them out. On the other hand, if an incentive plan can be gutted by some outside event, it makes very little motivational sense to take a purist view and let the chips fall where they may.

There may be a valid compromise position here. If a major uncontrollable external event has had an impact on profits—good or bad —the company could determine the impact and then adjust the profit budget or the results (on a pro forma basis) to recognize some, *but not all,* of that impact. For example, one company has adopted a set of principles similar to those embodied in its group medical insurance plan. It tells its division managers: At the end of the year, we will determine the profit impact of all the uncontrollable outside events that have occurred during the year. Then your original budget figure will be adjusted as follows: No adjustment will be given for that portion of the impact equal to 5 percent of your original profit budget. If the impact is greater, 75 percent of the extra impact will operate to reduce or increase your original profit budget. After such adjustment has been made, your results will be compared to the new budget figure and your bonus fund calculated accordingly.

This approach has merit because it offers some target relief in valid cases. But, like the medical insurance plan on which this approach is modeled, it may dissuade people from making spurious claims.

Another company took a more Machiavellian stance with its division managers: If you don't come to us for target relief, we will not impose higher budget figures on you in the event that some external event gave you an unplanned-for windfall. But the minute you show up to ask for any target relief, no matter how small, we reserve the right to review the favorable things that have happened, and you may end up with a net increase in your budget figure. This has quelled the temptation to scream about every little thing that goes wrong, because division managers really don't know whether top management is aware of the things that went right.

Determining Individual Awards

When overall bonus funds have been created and chunks of these funds have been allocated to various units of the company, the next step in the award process is to determine the amount of each eligible's award and to make special awards to deserving noneligibles.

Some companies pay awards on a group basis. Each eligible receives a proportionate share based on the relationship between his salary and the salaries of all other eligibles. This approach may encourage teamwork, but it may also encourage indolence as executives whose performance might otherwise be outstanding adjust their contributions to the lowest common denominator.

Moreover, the group award approach tends to magnify inequities in the company's current salary payments. For example, if one executive is making $40,000 but should be making $50,000, and another executive is making $40,000 but should be making $30,000, and both receive a 50 percent group award, the result widens the inequity between these executives from an initial figure of $20,000 to an ultimate figure of $30,000.

Other companies avoid the group award approach entirely and base awards solely on individual performance. Implicit in their choice is the assumption that if they motivate the individual, the teamwork will take care of itself. In any event, they will see to it that managerial backbiting doesn't become too pronounced.

Many of these same companies are deceiving themselves, however, when they say that they are truly rewarding individual performance. Two examples illustrate this fact.

A few years ago, a comprehensive survey of 12 companies' executive bonus plans was conducted. After asking how many people were eligible for bonus consideration, the following routine question was asked: "How many eligibles actually receive a bonus in a typical year?" Of the 12 companies asked, 9 had 90 percent or more of bonus eligibles; one had 86 percent; one had 75 percent; and one had 50 percent. It can be readily seen that these companies give most of their executives a bonus every year. Yet, in answer to an earlier question, every one of these companies stated that bonuses were awarded for outstanding performance only!

Because these results were puzzling, the companies were further asked: "If you give bonuses only for outstanding performance, how is it that such a high percentage of your eligible executives qualify each year?" After first appearing surprised at being asked such a question, most of the respondents gave a rather patronizing answer. "Well, it should be perfectly obvious," they said. "Our executives would never have made it to the positions they occupy if they weren't outstanding."

The Vertical Rating Flaw

This answer demonstrates a subtle but fundamental flaw in the manner in which many companies view their top management personnel. Certainly, these executives are outstanding—certainly, "the cream rises to the top"; but there are many grades of cream, and some are better than others. The only proper basis of performance assessment for an executive, therefore, is to compare him to his peers both in his own company and in others. On this basis, it is obvious that not every executive is outstanding. In fact, there is no reason to believe that executive performance, like the performance of other groups, is not distributed in a purely Gaussian manner. Accordingly, somewhere in the United States there have to be as many incompetent executives as there are outstanding ones.

What about the two companies in the survey with relatively reasonable percentages of eligibles receiving awards? Surely, here we have two examples of companies with enlightened management. Unfortunately, however, both companies had eligible lists numbering several thousand, and the data analysis indicated that the lower award frequency was coming out of the hides of the lowest-paid eligibles. In effect, better than 90 percent of the upper-level executives were receiving bonuses, but only around 25 percent of the lower-level executives were. Since the latter far outnumbered the former, the overall result made the company look good.

In another case, a company's bonus data showed what apparently was some evidence of performance discrimination. There was no one percentage of bonus for every executive—even when the effects of lower and higher salaries were factored out. The same applied to data from the previous year's bonus. Bonuses, however, were considerably lower in the current year than in the previous year. An examination of the funding formula showed that total bonus funds in the current year were only 60 percent of those generated in the previous year. Just for the fun of it, a few further checks were made, and these showed that every executive's bonus in the current year was precisely 60 percent of the bonus he received in the previous year. Thus, having rated each executive's relative performance contribution several years back, this company assumed that each executive was continuing to make precisely the same relative contribution every year.

These two illustrations show how hard it is to reward performance in a truly discriminating manner. Top managers in many companies grasp at any available rationalization to avoid making gutty performance assessments. They use the vertical rating error; or they increase or decrease individual bonuses from year to year only as the total amount of funds increases or decreases. Or they convince themselves that to withhold a bonus from an individual who has had one for several years running will either ruin his motivation or compromise his standard of living. In truly desperate cases, both reasons are advanced.

There is no simple answer to this problem. Only the implementation of a rational and valid performance appraisal system and a good dose of management guts will bring a solution.

One thing that a company should not do is allow the normal-award concept of allocation discussed earlier to spill over into the establishment of award ranges. For example, suppose a company has an award range of 30 to 60 percent of salary for a given class of executives. If the funds allocated to a given unit are not enough to produce a good award for each executive in this bracket (say 45 percent of salary), then the entire range of awards might be reduced proportionately. Thus, if the funds allocated are only enough to produce an average award of 30 percent of salary—a 33^1/3 percent reduction—the entire award range might be reduced by 33^1/3 percent and a new award range of 20 to 40 percent substituted.

A number of companies utilize this process, but it is generally wrong, because it assumes that every eligible will receive an award no matter how poorly the company performs.

In one division of a company, every eligible executive received an award one year. The smallest award was 3 percent of salary and the largest was 5 percent. The division manager was asked: "Why were your awards so small?" He replied, "Because we had a bad year in our division and the president gave us a tiny allocation."

He was asked another question: "Do you think that the difference between 3 percent of salary and 5 percent of salary adequately reflects the difference between your worst-performing and your best-performing executive?" "Oh, of course not," he said, "but you see, the funds were so small—what could I do?" It was then suggested, "Perhaps you could have given nothing to 15 out of your 20 eligible executives and used your entire allocation to grant significant rewards to just a few really outstanding individuals." "That's an interesting thought," he said, "but we *always* give everyone an award each year, so of course that idea simply wouldn't work."

Ranking the Eligibles

One approach that can be of assistance in determining individual awards is to rank all eligibles in descending order of their relative performance contributions. The word "relative" is key, for an individual who accomplishes less on an absolute basis than another but more in terms of what he *could have accomplished* would receive the higher ranking.

Having established the performance ranking, the executive making the award decisions starts from the top and works down. The individual ranked first receives an amount of bonus which when added to his salary will give him total compensation appropriate to this rating. (No reductions are ever made in bonus opportunities to reflect the size of the unit's allocation.) The same procedure is then followed for the second-ranked individual, the third, and so on until there are no funds left.

It is very likely that some individuals at the bottom of the list will receive no awards. And the smaller the amount of funds available for awards, the larger this group will be. Before making his final decision, however, the reviewer should consider whether there are one or two marginal cases just below the awards cutoff line who should perhaps receive the minimum award amount. If he decides in the affirmative, the reviewer will have to readjust the dollars assigned to various individuals above the cutoff to provide the necessary funds of these last one or two awards.

Therein lies the value of this procedure, for the executive making the award decisions is vividly reminded at every turn that the dollars required to give lower-ranked individuals any award at all in a year of less than fully outstanding unit performance will have to come out of the pockets of those whose performance contributions are considered greater. Recognizing this truth, the executive may be impelled to let the chips fall where they may, thereby increasing the motivational value of the company's bonus plan through the significant recognition that is implied in granting some executives maximum awards and others no awards at all.

Combination Group and Individual Awards

Some companies follow the policy of employing a combination of group and individual incentive awards in much the same manner that other companies weight divisional allocations with both the division's results and those of the corporation as a whole. In effect, the companies employing the combination approach seek to emphasize both teamwork and individual achievement and, in a way, obtain the best of both worlds.

Under this system, a given percentage of the overall fund (usually 20 to 50 percent) is distributed on a group basis. Every eligible executive receives this group distribution, which is usually prorated to salary. The remainder of the fund is then distributed on the basis of individual performance contributions.

If a company is going to employ a combination approach, the group award portion should really be prorated to award ranges and not to salary to avoid causing inequities. The range of awards, stated as a percentage of base salary, increases as the salary increases. Suppose, for example, that the highest range of awards, applicable to the president, was 30 to 90 percent of salary and the lowest range of awards was 10 to 30 percent of salary.

Suppose further that 25 percent of any funds generated was to be paid in the form of a group award. If the company has an outstanding year and a fund is generated sufficient to pay every eligible his maximum award, then the group award could—and should—consist of 25 percent of each eligible's award maximum. Thus the eligible with the highest award range would receive 22.5 percent of salary as a group award; and the eligibles with the lowest award range would receive 7.5 percent of salary.

If, on the other hand, the awards had been strictly prorated to base salary, every eligible would have received the same award percentage. As a result, the proportion of total award opportunity represented by the group award would unwittingly have been made significantly higher for the lowest-paid eligibles than for the highest-paid eligibles. Distributing group awards in proportion to the award ranges avoids these problems, although it does appear perhaps less democratic.

The proponents of the combination group-individual award approach, besides emphasizing its value in motivating both teamwork and individual achievement, believe that it may eliminate the tendency to water down awards. Everyone gets at least the group award, so the theory goes, and therefore top managers will see to it that only the good performers get anything more. Presumably they will have the guts to make this approach stick, because they can take comfort in the fact that the mediocre performer did get something. Of course, some of the monies appropriated for group awards might have been better spent on the outstanding performers, but nevertheless, the combination approach may have some definite merit if it can achieve its designer's objectives.

The integrated compensation structure and the philosophy of closing compensation gaps can be used profitably in plans featuring both group and individual awards. Essentially, the proper amount of individual award is the difference between the executive's base salary plus his group award and the position in his total compensation range that is appropriate for his performance contributions. However, a large group award granted in a year of outstanding corporate performance can, when combined with base salary, push the average-performing executive's total compensation beyond his appropriate range position. In such a case, no further individual bonus would be indicated.

A further advantage of the combination approach is its use as a transition device for the company that is moving from a purely group distribution plan to one based solely on individual performance. Typically, this company cannot make the switch overnight because it lacks the precision performance assessment infrastructure needed to support individually determined bonuses. But the company can adopt a combination plan, starting with, say, 90 percent of the funds distributed on a group basis and 10 percent on an individual basis. With each passing year, the group percentage can be decreased and the individual performance percentage increased until one day the company has almost painlessly achieved its initial objective. On its way down, the company may of course find some combination of group and individual awards that is particularly beneficial, and, if so, there is no reason for it not to stop right there.

Minimum Awards

Technically an executive should receive the exact amount of bonus necessary to raise his total compensation to his appropriate range position, but the amount should not be granted unless it is meaningful. A number of alternative approaches can be used to achieve this objective. For example, awards can be restricted to payments of at least 10 percent of salary; or 10 percent of salary but not less than $3,000; or a minimum 10 percent of salary for the lowest level of eligibles, tapering up to 20 percent for the highest level. All these approaches are workable; the best one considers organization size, salary distribution of the eligible group, and the range of bonus opportunities.

Automatic Awards for the Chairman and President

Awards for the chairman and president are particularly difficult to determine because there is usually a built-in conflict of interest. Although most companies have a committee of the board of directors assigned to approve incentive compensation awards, this committee is pretty much at the mercy of the top executives when it comes to receiving the data on which to base its decisions. Then again, the chairman and president are board members. Thus, determining awards for them is both difficult and often embarrassing for the individuals involved.

One way of resolving this problem is to provide for automatic awards to the chairman and president—unless the board deliberately acts to override the formula amount. Ultimately, the performance of the two top men is measured by the company's overall performance. And, since the company's overall performance determines the bonus funds that will be provided, it may make sense to tie the awards for the chairman and president to the corporate internal funding formula.

If aggregate norm bonuses are funded for meeting budget, for example, the chairman and president would receive their norm bonus amount when the company met its profit budget. By the same token, their bonuses would move up or down or would disappear according to the same funding formula.

Of course, it may be argued here that such an approach creates a patent conflict of interest. The divisions are motivated to submit low profit budgets so as to get the greatest bonus funding. And the CEO, knowing that he will automatically get an award, is motivated to accept those low profit budgets because they in turn will result in a low corporate budget. Such could certainly be the case, but there are usually a number of safeguards to prevent it from happening.

First, the corporate profit budget is generally approved by the board of directors, and presumably even the most somnolent board will come alive if the CEO's games-playing behavior becomes flagrant. Second, there is a stockholder-approved funding formula in operation, and a ridiculously low profit budget that does get by the board could run afoul of the limitations imposed by that formula. Third, as we shall see, most senior executives are given long-term incentives in addition to the incentives for annual performance. These long-term incentives are almost always geared to achieving absolute performance improvements, not performance relative to a budget or other management standard. The net result of approving low profit budgets and then barely achieving them may be to wipe out any payments under the company's long-term incentive plan, since absolute performance will probably be deplorable. Finally, the board or its compensation committee can override the automatic award feature if it would operate to produce an unfair award for the chairman or president.

Disposing of Surplus Bonus Funds

Another factor to consider in bonus formula design is the disposition of surplus funds that are not needed for bonuses in the current year. Such surpluses may accumulate because there aren't enough outstanding executives in an outstanding year to soak up the entire bonus fund. Or they may occur because the external funding formula was too liberal to begin with or has become too liberal over the years. Some companies restore such surpluses to net income and others retain them for use in future years.

Without viable internal fund generation formulas, surpluses should be restored to net income; if they are carried over to future years, management may yield to the temptation of using them as a means of equalizing executive bonuses from one year to the next, thereby reducing the differential between periods of excellent and poor corporate performance. On the other hand, carrying over surplus bonuses can be of assistance in unusual situations—for example, when one or two divisions in a company have such a disastrous year that they cancel out the funds generated by all—even the satisfactory —divisions.

With good internal fund-generating formulas which help to insure that bonus funds are used in a maximally motivating manner, there would appear to be no problem with the retention of surplus bonus funds from year to year.

Revising the External Formula

Formulas, like tires, do not last forever. Accordingly, a company's external funding formula should undergo periodic inspection to see whether it needs retreading or replacement.

Contrary to some executives' impressions, the company should not experience difficulty in finding the funds for awards to new eligibles—provided that the company's growth makes the addition of new eligibles justified. If the formula is predicated on return on stockholders' equity, a doubling of stockholders' equity and the maintenance of the same percentage return on that will yield double the funds. Since a doubling in company size is unlikely to warrant a doubling in the number of eligibles, the company may indeed be better off.

Another problem that may arise is that the industry may change its standards of performance. Suppose for example, the average return on stockholders' equity for an entire industry drops significantly over a period of years, owing perhaps to increased government regulation or a change in IRS rules concerning deductibility of business expenses or depreciation. In this event, the company will undoubtedly have trouble meeting the standards of previous years, and its bonus fund will be materially reduced. Yet, judged by the new industry standards, the company may be doing an excellent job.

The reverse can occur also. With rising industry standards of performance, the company's bonus plan is likely to become overfunded. Although this problem is not too hard to take, it should nevertheless be corrected before too much time has passed.

In cases such as these, the company may have to redesign its bonus formula. The procedure is identical to the one followed for the original formula. And, of course, the new formula should receive all the necessary tests, including a test on past company results, to insure that it is reasonable, produces meaningful award funds, and is well within the company's ability to pay.

Handling Bonus Erosion

The one bonus formula problem that cannot—and should not—be corrected through a change in the formula is lack of funds caused by an unjustified and significant increase in the number of eligibles. All bonus plans erode over time. Little by little, more and more people become eligible, and the number of special awards also rises. At first, the firm handles this erosion by cutting down the size of each bonus.

Eventually, this approach becomes counterproductive when the original group of eligibles starts complaining. It is at this time that management looks wistfully at its formula and thinks, "Just one little percentage point more on that multiplier would take care of all our problems." This is not an effective or even an ethical solution, because one of the reasons the formula was designed around industry performance standards was to control this very problem. Even today, a few companies use a funding formula which gives management a sort of "bonus bounty"—$5,000 for each regular eligible. Needless to say, the growth in the number of eligibles is about the only growth these companies seem to be achieving. The obvious, albeit painful, remedy for bonus erosion is to reduce the number of eligibles until sufficient funds are available to provide meaningful awards.

Time of Payment and Award Media

Having established the amount of award that a given executive is to receive, the company must also decide on the time and method of payment. Payment can be made in full at the time the award is declared or it can be deferred. (Deferred payments are considered later.)

In essence, the choice of payment media involves cash or something other than cash. And the something other than cash almost always is company stock—at least where immediate payments are concerned. There are usually no great advantages or disadvantages to either approach. The tax consequences are the same in both instances; the individual must pay full ordinary income tax rates on the cash received or on the market value of the stock as of the date it is paid to him.

Before 1964, ordinary income in the United States was taxed at rates as high as 91 percent. The Revenue Act of 1964 cut the maximum marginal tax rate to 70 percent, where it remained until the Tax Reform Act of 1969 established two classes of ordinary income for the first time. Income derived from personal services or, to put it more poetically, from the sweat of one's brow was to be considered *earned income,* while income produced from capital—such as interest, rents, dividends, and the half of capital gains taxed at ordinary rates—was to be considered *unearned income.*

Tax rates for earned and unearned income remain the same until the maximum rate hits 50 percent—currently $44,000 to

$52,000 of taxable income for the individual who is married and is filing a joint return. Then the rates diverge.

All earned income above $52,000 continues to be taxed at the 50 percent rate, but unearned income is taxed at the rates that were applicable to all ordinary income between 1964 and 1969: 53 percent on the next portion of income, 56 percent on the next, and so on until the maximum marginal rate of 70 percent is reached at more than $200,000 of taxable income.*

In the Tax Reform Act of 1976 Congress further changed the definition of earned income, of which more later. At the same time it also decided to rename earned income. Henceforth such income is to be called *personal service income,* and this new name is used in the remainder of these pages. The 50 percent maximum marginal tax still applies to all personal service income. And *all* bonuses, whether cash, stock, or coffee beans, are considered to be personal service income.

If company stock is used as the payment medium, the executive is generally free to convert his stock to cash at any time (unless unregistered shares are used, but this rarely occurs in immediate cash payments). If the award is entirely in company stock, the executive will probably cash at least part of it within a few months, inasmuch as the taxes on the entire award will come due shortly. For this reason, some companies prefer to give the executive a mixture of cash and company stock, such that the amount of cash paid is approximately equivalent to the amount of taxes on the entire award. With this approach, higher paid executives receive a greater proportion of cash because of the influence of the progressive tax structure.

Since the underlying hope in using company stock for an immediate bonus payment is that the executive will retain as much of it as possible, other companies prefer to pay the entire award in stock, recognizing that, although most executives will cash some of it for tax purposes, others may be able to meet their tax payments with outside income and retain all the stock.

If treasury shares are used, the choice between all stock and part

*As this manuscript was being prepared for publication, IRS attempted to simplify the preparation of tax returns for 1977. Previously, a married couple filing a joint return could itemize all deductions when such deductions exceeded the statutory $3,200 standard deduction allowed without itemization. Now, the couple can subtract from adjusted gross income only those itemized deductions *exceeding* this amount. However, IRS is increasing the taxable income brackets governing a given marginal tax bracket by the same $3,200. As a result, the net effect on actual tax liabilities will be zero. Because of this, many feel that this new approach is not, in fact, any simpler. Since IRS may soon revert to the time-honored methods of the past, the author has elected to ignore this recent change.

cash and part stock depends mainly on psychological factors. ("Treasury shares" here denotes both true treasury shares—those purchased on the open market some time prior to their delivery to the executive—and shares purchased on the open market and delivered directly to the executive. Both types cause the number of shares outstanding to remain unchanged, and therefore the two are similar for executive compensation purposes.)

Some top managers become visibly upset when an executive sells even one of his company shares, even for tax purposes. These companies should stay away from all-stock payments, because they create a conflict for the individual executive: He is damned by the company if he sells the shares, and he is damned by IRS if he doesn't and defaults on his tax payments. These companies should also stay away from *any* stock payments, because giving an individual ostensibly convertible securities and then imposing psychological pressure to render them unconvertible sharply reduces the motivational value of the bonus itself. Indeed, the individual may eventually have to terminate his employment in order to gain the use of the money tied up in company stock. (There are also legal restrictions applicable to the sale of shares by certain executives, and these must also be considered.)

If authorized but unissued shares ("new shares") are utilized, the same psychological factors remain but an additional factor is introduced. New shares increase the number of shares outstanding and therefore cause a dilution in earnings per share. True, this dilution occurs at the time the shares are delivered to the individual and the later act of sale by the executive is immaterial from an earnings-per-share standpoint. Even so, there is some evidence that company stockholders may be disturbed if there is a pattern of frequent sales. They feel, in effect, that the purpose of the plan has somehow been vitiated.

Nevertheless a company using new shares may elect to distribute the full bonus in company stock and risk stockholder dissatisfaction simply because it is strapped for cash. This is the only circumstance, in fact, in which the use of new shares would appear to be justified, because these shares have a double-barreled negative impact on earnings per share. First, the number of shares outstanding (the denominator in the earnings-per-share equation) is increased. Second, the after-tax earnings of the company (the numerator in the earnings-per-share equation) are reduced because of the charge for the bonus amounts. On the other hand, the company not only has avoided laying out any cash, but has actually received additional cash flow in the form of equity capital, since, like depreciation of capital facilities and equipment, it has charged the bonus payments to income but has incurred no actual expenditure. When treasury shares are utilized, there is only one negative effect on earnings per share and that occurs in the numerator: The company's after-tax earnings are reduced because of the deduction of the bonus amounts.

Stock Bonuses for Officers and Directors

Payment of bonuses in stock to corporate officers and directors can cause a problem, albeit a generally manageable problem. Section 16(b) of the Securities Exchange Act stipulates that if an officer or director makes a profit by selling shares within six months of purchasing the same or other shares, or makes a profit by purchasing shares within six months of selling the same or other shares, the profit must be returned to the company. Regulations interpreting the act define the transactions deemed to be purchases or sales in applying the six-month profit-return rule.

In general, the payment of company shares in satisfaction of a bonus is not considered a purchase by the Securities and Exchange Commission (SEC), but the subsequent sale of those shares *is* considered a sale. In such situations, therefore, the executive is ostensibly free to sell his bonus shares at any time. But it must be remembered that he might get hung up over the purchase of other shares. For example, suppose the executve receives a 1,000-share bonus in March and sells the shares in April, at which point the stock has a fair market value of $100 per share. If the executive also has a stock option on 1,000 shares at an option price of $50 per share, he will not be able to exercise the option (buy the shares) until at least six months after selling the bonus shares. But what if the option expires in five months?

Because of this provision in the law governing insider trading, companies have to take care that they are not putting their officers and directors in the untenable position of having profits from company stock but not being able to realize them because of the six-month holding period. And as can be seen, companies have to consider *all* their stock plans, not just a single plan, since two separate plans, each innocuous in itself, can combine to create a giant problem.

Telling the Individual of His Award

The last step in the bonus procedure is, of course, to inform the individual that he has received an award. In many companies, this is accomplished in a letter signed by the president and sent to the individual's home. The recipient is probably addressed by his first name even if the president has never met him or spoken to him.

The reason advanced for this procedure is to give the bonus plan greater prestige. A letter from the president makes the executive feel that he is on the inside and a part of the true management team. This may be valid, but for the same reason, one would think that the president would personally communicate the rationale for *not* granting an award, if such were the case. Of course, this rarely happens—it is the immediate boss who is given the task of bearing bad tidings.

Chances are that the president communicates directly with the award recipient to enhance not the bonus plan's prestige, but his personal prestige; after all, it's fun to play Santa Claus. Meanwhile, the president has undercut the individual's own supervisor, who made the initial recommendation that an award be granted, but may never have been informed as to the outcome. More than once, an executive, after receiving his award letter from the president, has gone to his boss to thank him, only to find that his boss was totally ignorant of the decision. ("Oh, so you got $10,000—well, that's just great!") After receiving such a reaction, the executive may well wonder if he should continue to look to his boss for his rewards. Some of the best "end runners" in the game of management first sharpened their skills on the company's bonus plan!

Some of the major principles involved in sound bonus plan design are these:

- Adopting meaningful award levels.
- Restricting regular eligibility to executives who have a *substantial* impact on the attainment of major company objectives.
- Providing for a few special awards to personnel not regularly eligible to participate.
- Designing an internal corporate funding formula to insure that the eligibles are motivated to accomplish what the company really wants accomplished.
- Designing an external corporate funding formula to act as a circuit breaker on the internal formula and assure the shareholders that amounts expended on executive bonuses will always be reasonable and in line with the company's ability to pay.
- Developing allocation procedures which recognize that some units outperform others. Better yet, designing individual unit

internal funding formulas to generate part of the funds for
that unit.

- Using the total integrated compensation range to establish bonus amounts, rather than paying bonuses as a percentage of
  base salary.

- Appraising executive performance realistically. Recognizing
  that in virtually every company there have to be some below
  average executives and seeing to it that they receive small
  awards or no awards at all.

- Always trying to grant outstanding personnel the award they
  deserve without regard to the size of the fund itself. Recognizing that dollars used to pay even token awards to mediocre
  executives usually come out of the pockets of the outstanding
  ones.

Deferred Compensation   5

Deferred compensation, as its name implies, is compensation earned in one year but paid in some future year. In its fullest application, deferred compensation covers payments made under company retirement, profit-sharing, and savings plans and even the payment of postretirement medical expenses. (Life insurance is of course the ultimate in deferred compensation!) This chapter, however, is restricted to the types of deferred compensation that are typically granted only to executive personnel. In tax parlance, these devices come under the label of nonqualified deferred compensation plans.

Deferred compensation for executives usually takes one of three forms: salary deferrals, bonus deferrals, or an employment agreement which provides for supplementary retirement payments (in addition to those provided under the company's qualified retirement, profit-sharing, or savings plans). Since bonus deferrals contain the greatest variety of design options, the greater part of this chapter has been given over to a detailed discussion of these deferrals.

Bonus Deferrals

Bonus deferrals can be grouped into two categories: short-term deferrals and long-term deferrals. Short-term deferrals involve paying part of the award at the time it is declared, with the remainder to be paid over the next few years. For example, a $10,000 award may be paid in five equal annual installments, consisting of $2,000 immediately and $2,000 in each of the next four years. The number of years that various companies use in their deferral cycles ranges from two to five. It should be noted, however, that the four- and five-year deferral cycles are the most common.

Long-term deferrals involve the postponement of the entire award until retirement or other termination of employment. Thereafter, the award is again typically paid in a series of equal annual installments, but in this case the deferral cycle is usually longer. Ten- to fifteen-year cycles are the most common.

Both motivational and tax reasons are cited as advantages of deferred compensation. (Tax reasons can of course be considered motivational if the executive bonus yields more after-tax income, but for discussion purposes they are considered separately.) Let us now take a look at the evidence.

Golden Handcuffs Revisited

As was stated earlier, the golden handcuffs approach is a negatively oriented motivational device which does not give the executive an incentive to remain with the company but rather gives him a "disincentive" to leave the company. The late social psychologist Kurt Lewin developed an ingenious "field theory" of motivation around principles operating in the physical world. He postulated that at any given point in time the individual is surrounded by both positive and negative motivational vectors and that the relative strength of these vectors dictates the direction in which the individual moves. Thus, if the positive vectors outweigh the negative ones, the individual moves in the direction indicated by the positive forces. Similarly, he would move in the direction of the negative vectors, if they were the stronger. The theory also posits that the individual remains immobilized if the positive and negative forces are equal. An interesting thing happened in some experiments, however. When the individual was confronted with both positive and negative forces of known and equal physical intensity, he did not remain immobilized but moved toward the positive force. In effect, the individual had a "set" to evaluate the positive forces as being worth more psychologically than physically.

So it may also be with money and deferred compensation. If a man is confronted with a positive force in the form of an offer from another company which will buy him out of the money he will lose by quitting and a negative force in the form of the golden handcuffs approach, he may well move to the other company even though the dollars involved are merely equal to and not more than he is losing. Moreover, in this instance he is subject to another psychological phenomenon—the grass is greener—and this may impel an even quicker movement in the "positive" direction.

Thus a company that wants to make a negatively oriented motivational device like golden handcuffs really work may find itself having to use an even greater amount of money than it otherwise might. But this is the start of a vicious circle, for the greater the deferred compensation, the easier it is to motivate the individual to accept an offer from another company. This is because his cash flow income is less than his nominal income, as mentioned earlier. For example, an executive with a base salary of $50,000 and a $25,000 bonus in five equal annual installments receives only $55,000 total cash flow during the first year of such an arrangement. He is obviously vulnerable to another company's offer of $75,000 with no deferrals. In the reverse situation, the company finds it difficult to attract a talented executive from a company which pays immediate cash bonuses.

Although the evidence on the efficacy of golden handcuffs is sparse, what does exist is not very encouraging. Some companies have tried and then abandoned the golden handcuffs approach, because it failed to retain outstanding personnel. In other companies, golden handcuffs are used with a vengeance. The air is heavy with the threat of discharge, and discharge, in these companies, carries a forfeiture of all unpaid deferred compensation installments. It is no coincidence that executives in these companies are characterized by passivity and an unwillingness to make gutty decisions that offer the possibility of becoming a hero, but also offer an equal possibility of being discharged at great financial sacrifice.

One claimed motivational advantage of golden handcuffs is its ability, in a short-term deferral application, to equalize an executive's income from year to year. This was an advantage years ago when short-term deferrals first got started in American industry, but it may not be an advantage any longer.

Credit for initiating short-term deferrals is generally given to the automobile industry, which is characterized by huge bonuses relative to base salary and substantial fluctuations in year-to-year profits. Thus bonuses that are huge one year may be minuscule the next. And, if a bonus is paid consistently for some years, executives come to depend on at least part of it to maintain their standard of living.

Without an income-averaging provision in the tax laws, as was the case prior to 1964, the payment of a huge bonus one year and a small bonus the next was terribly inefficient from a tax standpoint because the huge bonus was hit with extremely high marginal tax rates (up to 91 percent in those days). Thus, when it was first initiated, the short-term deferral cycle made a good deal of sense.

Today the executive can take advantage of the income-averaging provision or of the 50 percent maximum tax on personal service income, whichever gives him a better deal. In either case, from a tax standpoint he is protected against wild year-to-year income swings. Moreover, most industries neither pay bonus awards of the magni-tude of the auto industry nor experience quite the same degree of year-to-year profit fluctuation.

In fact, there is one school of thought which argues that short-term deferrals, through their year-to-year equalization of income, actually provide diminished motivation because they dilute the impact of an exceptionally good year followed by an exceptionally poor one. For example, the individual who receives a $25,000 bonus in each of four years under a five-year short-term deferral will still receive $20,000 in the fifth year, even if he receives no new awards that year because his performance is poor. Conversely, if his performance is superb, and his bonus in the fifth year is doubled to $50,000, his cash flow that year will be only $30,000—$20,000 from his previous four bonuses and the first installment of $10,000 from his current bonus. Thus the difference between superb and poor performance is a cash flow of $30,000 versus $20,000, not $50,000 versus zero, as in the nominal bonus amounts.

Although it is true that no one has proved that the short-term deferral approach diminishes motivation, it is equally true that the advantages of equalizing income from year to year are lost after a number of years in the company's deferral cycle. Thus an individual who receives a $25,000 bonus for five years under a five-cycle short-term deferral receives $25,000 cash flow in the sixth year and each year thereafter as long as he continues to receive additional $25,000 awards. His cash flow compensation then equals his nominal compen-sation, and little further advantage accrues from the use of short-term deferrals.

This does not necessarily mean that the company should not employ any holding devices. Some executives—particularly the youn-ger ones—may indulge in impulsive behavior which they later regret. A modest amount of holding power may therefore be desirable to curb these impulsive acts and at least make the executive think twice. But such holding power is already supplied by forfeiture provisions in the company's retirement, profit-sharing, and savings plans and by benefits that are related to length of service, such as vacations. These are enough to make one think.

It is correct to say that a person is *motivated* to hand over his wallet to someone holding a gun on him. The same sort of negative motivation is implied by the golden handcuffs approach. An alternative approach, designed to stress the symbiotic aspects of the employee-employer relationship, obviously therefore seems to be far more preferable.

Perhaps the best way to summarize the arguments against golden handcuffs is to recount the experience one company president had when, at the annual stockholders meeting, he introduced a new bonus plan incorporating this feature. He gave an impassioned speech extolling the virtues of the new plan and said it would materially aid the company in attracting and especially in retaining capable executives. When he was finished, one of the world's most famous dissident stockholders rose and said, "Mr. President, I have listened to your remarks with great interest and am happy to learn how your new plan will attract and retain capable executives. Now, sitting three places from your left is an individual whom my proxy statement identifies as Mr. Jones. He is a vice-president of your company and president of its XYZ division. Mr. President, if I recall, I first saw Mr. Jones at the annual meeting of the ABC company some four years ago. He was a vice-president of that company and was being paid a large deferred bonus to attract and retain him. Then about two years ago, Mr. President, I again saw Mr. Jones. This time he was vice-president of the DEF company and was again being paid a large deferred bonus to attract and retain him. I have only one question, Mr. President. Where will Mr. Jones be two years from now?"

It is a good question.

Individualization of Deferrals

Individualization of the compensation package is one good answer. Here, the individual is not made to take something he doesn't want but instead is offered the chance to take something he definitely wants. Obviously, if he decides to defer some or all of his bonus, no strings should be attached to his choice; and he should be permitted to receive *all* his funds when he resigns—whatever the reason. Since the executive will probably choose the type of compensation which is most appealing to him at that particular moment—and hence highly motivating—and since not every company is employing the individualization approach, its use can give a company a significant edge over the competition in attracting, retaining, and motivating executive personnel.

Tax Consequences of Short-Term Deferrals

Now let us turn to the tax consequences of short-term deferrals. Ostensibly, the executive gains a tax advantage by spreading his bonus over a number of years and thereby equalizing his income. The top slice of this income will presumably attract a lower marginal ordinary income tax rate than a large bonus all in one year.

There are several factors working against such an advantage, however. First, as noted earlier, there is an income-averaging provision in the current income tax law, as well as the 50 percent maximum tax rate, and either helps the executive avoid the higher taxes associated with unusual swings in total compensation. Second, since the payment installments under a short-term deferral are made while the individual is still employed, and since his salary is unlikely to go in any direction but up (especially in an inflationary environment), the executive may well find himself paying a higher marginal tax rate on the last few installments of any award than would have been the case had he received it in a lump sum.

Third, tax rates themselves might rise. Certainly, federal rates have fallen in recent years. But there has been a distinct tendency for state and local income taxes to rise and fill the void. To the extent that tax rates rise, the value of deferring income will be offset.

Fourth and finally, if the deferred monies are not invested, the individual is certain to suffer a penalty from short-term deferrals. After all, he could have taken the monies immediately, paid his taxes on them, and put them to work. Surprisingly, many companies with short-term deferral plans do not invest the money being held for future distribution. For them, such an approach is a good deal, and in fact they may be able to earn enough on the retained capital to pay for the entire cost of the last few installments. For the individual executive, however, such an approach is no deal at all.

To the company, the tax consequences of short-term deferrals are simple. The company can deduct deferred amounts on its income tax returns but only when they are actually paid to the individual.

Tax Consequences of Long-Term Deferrals

A more compelling case can be made for the tax advantages of long-term deferrals, but the road is uncertain in this area also.

The reason most often advanced as to why long-term deferrals are advantageous is that the individual will probably be earning less after retirement and thus will have a lower marginal tax bracket for additional ordinary income. Hence, deferred amounts taken after retirement seemingly have a good chance of being taxed at a lower rate than would be the case had they been received immediately.

Interestingly, this argument has been strengthened by a change introduced into the Tax Reform Act of 1976. When Congress passed the Tax Reform Act of 1969 and first subdivided ordinary income into two classes, it stipulated that for income to be considered personal service income, two tests would have to be met. First, as discussed earlier, the income would have to be received for services rendered. Second, it would have to be received by the end of the tax year following the tax year in which it first no longer was subject to a substantial risk of forfeiture. Unless *both* requirements were met, the income would not be considered personal service income and hence could be taxed at rates as high as 70 percent. This second stipulation had the effect of converting income out of the personal service category if, say, the executive opted to defer receipt of his bonus until his retirement ten years later and if the eventual receipt of the bonus was not subject to forfeiture in the event that he terminated his employment prematurely.

Under the Tax Reform Act of 1976 Congress struck down this second stipulation. Now all income for services rendered will be considered personal service income, no matter when it is received and no matter whether any strings are attached to its eventual receipt.

These points notwithstanding, there are several pitfalls in the broader argument that deferring income always results in tax savings. First, the test as to whether tax rates are indeed lower must be made between the year in which the bonus was initially declared and the year in which the installment is received—not between the last year of employment and the first year of retirement. On this basis, it may turn out that the individual has no tax advantage at all. For example, suppose a man with a $30,000 salary had some bonus money deferred until after his retirement. Suppose further that the company has a final-pay retirement plan which provides a benefit equal to 50 percent of the last year's salary. If the deferral occurred early in the man's career and his salary had meanwhile advanced to $80,000 per year, he would retire with annual payments of $40,000 per year from the retirement plan and would thus be in a higher bracket for additional ordinary income than he was way back in the year in which the money was deferred.

And remember that this pattern can occur even though the individual never receives another promotion. Increases in productivity push up going rates of compensation and so does high inflation. Given the inflationary trends of the early 1970s, it looked for a while as though even first-level foremen might soon be making $1 million per year.

Then, too, there is the matter of outside income. This obviously has a tendency to rise as the individual grows older and hence may represent a significant portion of his postretirement income. Because of this, the individual actually has to be receiving substantially lower company retirement income when the installment is paid than he received in salary when the award was first declared before there can be any advantage at all.

The impact of tax rates and tax laws on deferrals should not be overlooked. Long-term deferrals involve a long period of time, during which taxes may rise. The extent of the rise will determine whether long-term deferrals will be seriously eroded. And if Congress should act again to change the rules governing deferred compensation, this could deal an especially serious blow to long-term deferrals, which depend heavily for their tax efficacy on the assumption that the individual's tax rates will be reduced.

Government Tax Money as Investment Capital

There is, however, one very important tax advantage to deferred compensation, and this is the executive's ability to use government tax money—the amounts he would have paid as taxes had he taken the income immediately—as investment capital. Assume, for example, that a 45-year-old executive who received a $50,000 bonus immediately would have to turn over 50 percent of it—or $25,000—to the government. He would be left with $25,000 which he could invest. Assume further that he invests his $25,000 in such a way that he receives no dividends or interest for the 20 years prior to his retirement but does increase his original investment to $100,000—a fourfold appreciation. He therefore has a long-term capital gain of $75,000.

Assume again that the executive's marginal tax bracket for additional ordinary income drops to 40 percent after his retirement and that he sells only a portion of his investment each year. Therefore, he can expect to be taxed at a rate of only 20 percent on long-term capital gains and can keep at least 80 percent of his total appreciation. His after-tax proceeds will therefore be $85,000, consisting of his original $25,000 investment and 80 percent of his $75,000 appreciation.

Suppose, however, the original award of $50,000 was deferred and invested in the very same securities. No tax is payable until the securities are handed over to the executive, and therefore the entire $50,000 is put to work. Since it was invested in the same securities, it will also quadruple in value, appreciating to a total of $200,000 by the time the executive retires. The full value of these securities is taxable at ordinary income tax rates when distributed to the individual, but, by taking it over a period of time, he can hope to maintain a 40 to 50 percent postretirement bracket for additional ordinary income. Thus he stands to retain 50 to 60 percent of the $200,000 of deferred compensation—or $100,000 to $120,000. This represents a very substantial increase over the $85,000 he would have received by paying his taxes at once and going for a long-term capital gain.

The use of government tax money as investment capital presupposes, of course, that the deferred compensation will be invested. Surprisingly, a good many companies do not invest deferred compensation, or if they do, they do not give the executive the benefit of any appreciation. Thus the $10,000 that is deferred when the executive is age 40 is the same $10,000 that will be paid him after he reaches age 65. Meanwhile, tax rates may have risen, and the executive will have lost the opportunity to put his money to work. During the same period, inflation, which is seemingly endemic in this country, will have had plenty of time to work its special magic on the purchasing power of the original $10,000. Therefore, unless deferred compensation is invested, the executive not only is not better off, but is far worse off than he would have been if he had taken the money immediately.

Investment Media

There is no single investment medium for deferred compensation funds that is best for everyone, but the length of time involved in long-term deferrals suggests the use of some sort of equity security to provide protection against the ravages of inflation. Some companies use fixed income securities, and others guarantee the individual the same rate of interest on his funds as the company itself pays to borrow money. But the most common practice among those who do invest deferred compensation monies is to place them in company stock. Being an equity security, company stock seemingly protects against inflation and may offer some additional on-the-job motivation—the executive is naturally interested in protecting his investment.

The only problem with company stock is that the executive, what with his stock options and his profit-sharing and savings plan proceeds, runs the risk of becoming "company stock poor." In terms of sound investment practice, such an event is undesirable in any company; in some companies it is particularly undesirable, because the company's stock cannot, by the wildest stretch of anyone's imagination, be considered to have the stability that characterizes a sound long-term growth vehicle.

As a result of these problems with company stock, a few companies offer their executives an opportunity to place deferred compensation monies in equities of other issuers, either in a diversified portfolio selected by company officers or the company's bank or in a mutual fund. From an investment standpoint, this sort of opportunity makes a good deal of sense, especially when it is coupled with at least some amount of company stock. On the other hand, some company presidents fear that such an approach will bring a withering blast of criticism from the shareholders, who may feel that management, through its purchase of equities of other issuers, has vividly demonstrated its lack of confidence in its own stock.

If outside securities are selected by management, there is the further problem that the company will be blamed for investment losses or will at the least be subject to the deprecations of Monday morning quarterbacks. Most companies use outside advice for this reason.

The use of outside securities can bring a company both tax and cost problems. Suppose the company buys 100 shares of IBM for the executive at $300 per share. Whether it later sells the shares at $600 per share to pay off the executive or gives him the 100 shares, it will be subject to a capital gains tax on the $30,000 gain. It would not be subject to such a tax, however, if it used its own securities. What is to be done?

Bearing the additional tax on the IBM shares increases the company's costs of providing deferred compensation. On the other hand, charging the executive for the additional tax will probably wipe out his tax advantage and then some. Alternatively, the company could avoid any capital gains tax by giving the executive a phantom investment in IBM, in effect offering to pay him at retirement a sum of cash equal to the then current value of 100 IBM shares. But in this case the company has to defray from its own pocket, not simply the tax on the gain, but the whole gain.

For these reasons, most companies employing long-term deferrals stick to offering a choice of cash with interest or investment in the company's shares. If the executive opts for stock, the company reinvests any dividends in more deferred company shares by dividing the amount of the dividends by the fair market value per share as of the date when the dividend is declared.

Deferred Compensation Contracts

Sometimes, instead of being geared to the company's bonus plan, deferred compensation takes the form of individual executive contracts which specify that certain postretirement payments be made. Usually these contracts provide that the executive must actually retire from the company ("If you remain until retirement, you will receive $25,000 per year for the remainder of your life") or are geared to his length of service ("For each year of service, you will receive a single payment of $25,000 after your retirement"). In addition, it is common practice to require that the executive, as a condition of receiving the money, either refrain from joining a competitor after his retirement, or hold himself available as a consultant, or both. These conditions are golden handcuffs of a sort, but they are so relatively mild as to be insignificant. It is rare that an executive would join a competitor after his retirement; and, if he never seems to be available for consultation, the company probably wouldn't object because it is not likely to call him anyway!

These conditions are essentially included to avoid any conflict with the IRS doctrine of constructive receipt, which is discussed shortly. It is ironic, however, that use of the consulting requirement in particular has caused the Social Security Administration in some cases to claim that the individual's deferred compensation payments represent income from gainful employment (consulting), hence unwittingly invalidating the executive's claim to social security benefits.

For all practical purposes, therefore, the deferred compensation contained in individual employment contracts is not substantially different from that obtained under a bonus plan, except that the latter form of compensation may, if the plan is soundly designed, be better related to the individual's performance than the former, which ultimately represents compensation for staying alive and out of trouble.

Tax Consequences to the Company

As with short-term deferrals, the company does not receive a tax deduction on long-term deferred compensation payments until they are actually made. At that time, the company can deduct the full value of the payment, including all appreciation above the original amount deferred. (Of course, if the value has declined below the original amount contributed, the company loses part of its deduction.)

Accounting reserves can be established for deferred compensation monies but generally they cannot be formally funded, with payments guaranteed to the executive by some agency outside the company. A few companies tried to establish deferred trusts for their executives, but IRS held that such a company was not entitled to a deduction at the time the money was deposited in the trust, assuming the money could later be forfeited by the executive (for example, in the event that he resigned voluntarily before retirement). Furthermore, if a trust was established and no conditions were imposed on the ultimate transfer of the monies to the executive, he would have immediate income and would be taxed on it as such.

Therefore, deferred compensation monies generally must remain unfunded, so they constitute a sort of lien on the company. Because of this, the executive could lose his entire deferred monies if the company should eventually go bankrupt. Such an event actually happened in the celebrated Penn Central case.

Individualizing the Deferred Compensation Plan

As noted earlier, a more motivational approach to deferred compensation is to let each eligible executive decide what he wants to do with his money and, if he elects to defer it, to grant him that election without imposing golden handcuffs restrictions.

As an example, the executive might elect to defer what subsequently turns out to be a $10,000 bonus. In addition to specifying the portion of his bonus to be deferred, the executive might also be allowed to choose the manner in which the deferred funds were to be invested (cash with interest or company stock) and the disposition of dividends and interest (either payment to him as declared or reinvestment in the media from which the monies were generated). Finally, he might also choose the year in which the repayment of the deferred monies (plus any appreciation thereon) would commence and the number of annual installments in which the entire amount would be paid.

A plan of this type does involve some administrative expense, but it is usually only a tiny fraction of the total amount being deferred. And, since the executive is receiving the types of compensation he prefers, the potential motivational benefits to be derived from an individualized approach far outweigh the meager costs involved.

One potential pitfall should be mentioned. Under IRS regulations, deferred compensation cannot be counted as compensation for purposes of determining (1) a pension payment under a qualified pension plan or (2) a contribution under a qualified profit-sharing plan. If benefits or contributions are predicated on base salary, the executive who defers some of his base salary therefore stands to forfeit some eventual retirement income and this may defeat any tax advantage he had hoped to gain. The same can apply if benefits or contributions are predicated on total cash compensation and the executive defers some or all of his bonus.

In a number of companies this problem can be circumvented. First, in companies that do not include bonuses in their definition of pensionable earnings or of compensation for profit-sharing plan purposes, the executive can defer his bonuses without worry. Second, even if bonuses are included, the company's pension plan may be predicated on, say, five-year final average total cash compensation. In that case the executive can defer up until the fifth year before retirement without affecting his pension.

Nevertheless, this aspect bears close examination when designing deferred compensation alternatives.

The Doctrine of Constructive Receipt

The types of choices just described, while highly motivational, will be self-defeating if the executive has to pay full and immediate taxes on his entire award at the time it is deferred. This will be the penalty if the company or the executive runs afoul of the IRS doctrine of constructive receipt. In effect, an individual is presumed to have income at any time he can—to quote IRS—"reach out his hand and take it." Thus, if the company were to say to the executive, "You're going to receive a $10,000 award; what do you want to do with it?" and the executive were to reply, "Defer it," the money would be duly deferred. But meanwhile, the executive would have to ante up the taxes on the entire award by the next April 15. When the company announced the bonus, he could have taken it, and the fact that he didn't is immaterial because as IRS also says, "A taxpayer cannot turn his back voluntarily on income."

The doctrine of constructive receipt, like the Monroe Doctrine, is conceptually clear but not always easy to apply. As a result, some time ago IRS published five case histories to illustrate which types of deferred compensation would breach the doctrine of constructive receipt and which would not. While IRS's intentions were entirely honorable, it only added to the confusion, for there seemed to be no discernible logic running through all five of the case histories. As an additional "service," therefore, it consented to make advance rulings on deferred compensation plans.

Although there are no hard and fast rules in the area of constructive receipt, it does appear that an executive can voluntarily defer nonforfeitable compensation payments if he elects to do so sufficiently in advance of the time when the compensation is actually earned. It is even more helpful if the executive, at the time he makes the election, is uncertain as to what the compensation will eventually be. Thus, on January 1, at least one year prior to the date of a bonus award, the executive might give the company a statement that reads: "I don't know whether I am going to receive a bonus 14 months from now, and, if I do receive one, I don't know what the amount will be, but should a bonus be awarded to me, I would like to defer 75 percent of it until my retirement or other termination of employment."

Generally speaking, the more time between the date an election to defer is filed and the date the compensation is actually earned, the less likely it is that the executive will encounter problems with the Internal Revenue Service.

Because of the uncertainties surrounding the doctrine of constructive receipt, a company considering an individualized deferred compensation plan should never venture forth without a Bible in one hand and a very competent tax lawyer in the other.

Recently, IRS issued the ominous notice that it would no longer supply advance rulings to specific companies concerning the tax status of their deferred compensation programs. Then, in February 1978, IRS proposed a new revenue ruling. If adopted, it would require an executive who was given a choice of taking income when earned or of deferring it to pay tax on that income in the year that it was first earned, notwithstanding its payment at some later date and notwithstanding that the deferred income might be subject to a future forfeiture under certain conditions. Assuming both that this ruling is finally adopted and that its legality is upheld by the courts, *voluntary* deferrals—by executives or anyone else—will be dead. However, the odds do not seem to favor the position of IRS. Numerous past cases have touched on the issues involved here, and in virtually every case IRS has come up the loser.

Accounting Consequences of Deferred Compensation

The initial value of deferred compensation is charged against the company's reported pretax earnings in the year the executive performed the services that gave rise to the compensation. Thus if a bonus of $10,000 is earned for 1977 performance, it is charged off totally in 1977, even though the executive receives only a part or none of it immediately.

As noted earlier, the company is not entitled to deduct a deferred compensation payment on its income tax return until the payment is made to the executive. This would seem to leave the company in the untenable position of reducing pretax income by $10,000, reducing the provision for federal income taxes by zero, and hence reducing aftertax income by the same $10,000, instead of the $5,200 reduction that would normally be expected.

However, in requiring the company to take the $10,000 pretax charge to its reported earnings, the accountants also let the company show the lowered provision for federal income taxes that would result if the deferred compensation were paid immediately. Assuming a 48 percent marginal tax rate, the company thus lowers its reported pretax earnings by $10,000, its reported provision for federal income taxes by $4,800, and hence its reported aftertax earnings by $5,200.

Naturally, the company's *actual* tax bill has not been lowered by this $4,800 and will not be until the $10,000 is actually paid to the executive. To reconcile this discrepancy, the accountants have the company enter an IOU for $4,800 in a balance sheet account called deferred income taxes. Then, when the $4,800 tax relief is actually received, the IOU for that amount is cancelled. The $4,800 sum does not flow through the income statement at that later time.

Now, suppose this $10,000 bonus is deferred in cash with interest compounded at the prime rate. The principal sum has already been charged to earnings, as just shown, but the interest accruals will have to be charged to earnings as they are made. Once again, the company will show in its annual report the tax relief it would have received had the accrual been immediately deductible. And once again, an IOU will be entered in the deferred income tax account in the balance sheet.

If the $10,000 bonus is deferred in company stock, the rules are more complex. To illustrate let us assume that the company's stock is selling for $100 per share at the time the deferral is made, which means the individual's deferral account is credited with 100 shares. Let us further assume, for the sake of simplicity, that no dividends are paid during the deferral period, but that the stock rises to $200 per share by the time it is delivered.

Initially, the accounting aspects are the same as those for a cash deferral of $10,000. The company charges its reported pretax earnings by $10,000, shows the reduced provision for federal income taxes, and enters an IOU for $4,800 in its deferred income tax account. However, in determining its earnings per share during the deferral period the company must include the extra 100 shares in its share base. It is allowed to use the so-called treasury share method of accounting, though.

To illustrate, let us look at the year when the deferral was made. The company charged its reported pretax earnings with $10,000 but didn't lay out any cash; thus its stockholders' equity account rises by $10,000 (compared with what would have happened had the bonus been paid immediately in cash), which amount is exactly equal to the initial market value of the 100 shares.

Ostensibly, in determining earnings per share the company would have to lower the numerator of the equation (aftertax earnings) by $5,200, representing the aftertax effect of the $10,000 bonus, and it would have to increase the denominator of the equation (shares outstanding) by 100, representing the ultimate promise of 100 shares. But the company is permitted to adopt the following line of reasoning: We will eventually have to issue 100 shares, but we have also created $10,000 of additional stockholders' equity. If we wished, on the date we credited the shares to the executive's account we could use this extra $10,000 of stockholders' equity to buy in 100 shares of stock from the open market. In that case, we would keep the number of shares outstanding from increasing. Hence, the only charge to earnings per share we will show will be in the numerator (aftertax earnings will decrease by $5,200), and the number of shares outstanding will be the same. So, when all is said and done, the accounting for a deferral in shares is, at least initially, the same as that for a deferral in cash.

Accounting for Appreciation

Now we come to the year of payout, when the shares have appreciated in value to $200 each. First, the company is finally permitted to take a tax deduction on its income tax returns. The deduction in this case is $20,000, representing the then current value of the 100 shares. In turn, this reduces the company's actual income taxes for the year by 48 percent of $20,000, or $9,600. As indicated earlier, the first $4,800 of this $9,600 reduction in taxes goes into the deferred income tax account to cancel out the IOU deposited there when the deferral was made. But what about the remaining $4,800?

Not many years ago, some companies decided they should let this additional $4,800 flow through their income statement that year, making the reported provision for federal income taxes decline by $4,800. This would have made the reported aftertax income *increase* by $4,800, since the accountants required no further charge to pretax earnings beyond the original $10,000 that was charged at the time the deferral was made.

Obviously, the accountants didn't like what was happening, so they propounded the following rule: The value of a tax deduction with respect to a compensation payment may be used to reduce the reported provision for federal income taxes only to the extent that the compensation payment itself is charged to reported pretax earnings. To the extent it is not, such value will bypass the income statement and be deposited directly into the balance sheet as an additional contribution to stockholders' equity. Since the $10,000 of appreciation in the shares was never charged to reported pretax earnings, neither will the $4,800 of tax relief generated by deducting this $10,000 of appreciation. Instead, the $4,800 will increase stockholders' equity by a like amount, in the same manner that the original $10,000 did.

Now we come to the moment of truth. The company pays the executive his 100 shares. Clearly, there is no further playing around with the treasury share method of accounting, because the shares have actually been issued and must be included in the share base in figuring earnings per share. However, the company still has the additional $10,000 of stockholders' equity created when the shares were promised, and now it has a further $4,800 in stockholders' equity stemming from the tax relief generated on the additional $10,000 in appreciation. Thus it can, if it wishes, use this $14,800 to buy back shares from the open market. Since the shares are now worth $200 each, the company can buy back 74 shares from the open market, leaving 26 shares still outstanding. Whether the company actually buys back those shares of course depends on whether it has unneeded equity capital or whether it can use the $14,800 for some internal investment.

During the time between the original deferral and the actual payout to the executive, the company must continue to follow the aforementioned treasury method in determining whether any net extra shares should be added to its share base in determining the year's true earnings per share. In making this calculation, however, it is allowed to pretend that it already has the extra contribution to stockholders' equity that would be generated through deductibility of the appreciation. Of course, if the shares appreciate for a while and then depreciate, the company gets to lower the net extra shares in its share base. However, the company is not allowed to show a negative net number of extra shares in the event the share value declines below its value at the time the original deferral was made.

We can now begin to see that the cost of compensation can be recorded in more than a single way. In this particular transaction, the company took a charge to its earnings for the original deferral. It also increased its shares outstanding by at least 26 at the end of the deferral period, and these extra 26 shares will serve to dilute future earnings per share in every year the company remains in business. If it wished, it might have increased its shares outstanding by as many as 100, but in so doing it would have created extra equity capital just as if it had sold these extra shares to the investing public.

Earlier we assumed that no dividends were payable on the deferred shares during the deferral period, but that is generally not the case. Here, the original value of the dividend is charged to earnings in exactly the same manner as an interest payment on a cash deferral. The charge occurs when the dividend is paid. If the dividends are then invested in more deferred shares, the appreciation in such shares is treated like the appreciation in the original shares—in other words, there is no charge to earnings, but the number of shares outstanding increases.

One final point. Suppose the deferred shares had some strings attached, such as forfeiture in the event of premature termination, and suppose that the executive quit prematurely and the shares were forfeited. What then? The answer is simple. Since the company has already charged these shares to its earnings, it merely takes a credit to earnings in the same amount and in the year the termination occurs. The balance sheet entry for deferred income taxes is also reversed at this time.

Personal Financial Planning

Contrary to common belief, there has not been an automatic tax advantage to deferred compensation payments for many years. But now we have a number of progressive companies granting the executive options as to how his compensation is to be paid.

Unless he is a tax lawyer how can the executive make an intelligent choice? For that matter, how is he going to find sufficient time to manage his outside investments, considering the ever increasing demands of his company? The sad result is that many executives, even those concerned with company finance, neglect their own personal planning and miss significant opportunities to increase their net worth.

These executives do not lack for advice, but unfortunately most of it is somewhat biased. The mutual fund salesman or the life insurance salesman will be only too happy to perform a detailed analysis of the executive's personal finances, but the recommendations will more than likely involve healthy investments in mutual funds or life insurance.

As a result, separate companies or specialized sections of consulting firms and banks have recently been created to help the executive in his personal financial planning. Groups of experts skilled in various types of investments analyze the executive's total financial picture and provide him with unbiased advice. The advice is truly unbiased because the fee for this service depends on the total assets being analyzed; these groups do not receive brokerage fees, life insurance commissions, or the like.

Some companies pay for this type of service, because they see it as a cheap way of obtaining more of the executive's time and energy. And because an outside service is involved, the company can stay out of the executive's personal financial affairs.

Properly designed deferred compensation plans can have both motivational and tax advantages. But neither advantage is automatic. Deferred compensation in particular is likely to motivate only to the extent that it appeals to the individual executive. Even the most clear-cut tax advantage is worth little if the executive has an urgent need for current income. Yet there are few clear-cut tax advantages in the area of deferred compensation.

Therefore two basic principles should be followed in making intelligent use of deferred compensation:

1. Carefully analyze the tax consequences of various deferred compensation alternatives. Never assume that, just because other companies have adopted a given practice, it is necessarily tax-advantageous.
2. Give the executive a choice. Don't force him to take deferred compensation—no matter how advantageous it may appear. And, above all, don't adopt the golden handcuffs approach, for it is likely to motivate the wrong people into staying with the company.

Long-Term
Incentives
Based on
Market Price _____ 6

If a company gives its executives a strong incentive to maximize annual profits, what more does it need to do other than to provide such fringe benefits as pension plans, then get about its business?

To shed some light on this question, let's contrast two businesses. The first is that of a pretzel vendor on New York's streets. Every day the pretzel vendor makes five decisions (to the extent he has a choice):

1. He decides from whom he will buy his pretzels.
2. He decides on the price he will pay.
3. He decides how many pretzels he will buy.
4. He decides where he will locate his cart.
5. He decides on a selling price.

The business of pretzel vending may be unromantic, but it is also comforting, because the pretzel vendor knows the results of his five decisions by the end of the day.

In contrast, take the case of the petrochemical business. After careful analysis, the president of a petrochemical company decides to build a new plant. Since there are tremendous economies of scale in petrochemicals, he decides there is no point in fooling around: The new plant must be huge. So the company commits $750 million, starts looking around for land, and hires architects and engineers. If the company is lucky and too many things don't go wrong, the new plant

will be ready for its first tryouts in five or six years. Then, after a
shakedown period of a year or so, it will be ready to start churning out
products.

What if there is a glut of such products on the market by that
time? Or what if energy prices have increased to such a degree that
cost assumptions have been thrown into a cocked hat? Or what if the
great new product that the plant was designed to produce is greeted
by yawns from the consuming public? (Witness the case of Corfam.)
In cases like these the company will lose a pile of money, not because
of a current decision but because of a decision made some six years
earlier. And don't forget that between the time when it was decided to
build the plant and the time when the plant went on stream there
were no revenues accruing from this decision. There were only costs:
costs for architectural and engineering talent, costs for land and materials, and so on.

If the president of our hypothetical petrochemical company had
been given only one incentive, to produce annual profits, he might
well have decided that it was in his own economic interests not to build
the new complex. Profits would then have been higher during the
next six years and his bonuses would have been greater. While he was
at it, the president could also have cut out spending for research and
development and for management development, and he could have
halved the advertising budget while shaving product quality and deferring maintenance on equipment. Then the profits would have
been greater yet and his bonuses might have risen to awesome
proportions.

Of course, the company might go out of business in five to seven
years, since costs would have skyrocketed because of aging and poorly
maintained plant and equipment, and since no new products would
have been streaming out of the empty research labs, and since some
customers would have stopped buying the company's products because of deteriorating quality, and since other customers would have
forgotten the company's products because they were no longer adver-
tised much, and since poor managers would have risen to high positions. By that time, bonuses under the annual incentive plan would
have plummeted to zero, and presumably the short-sighted president
would finally have received his just rewards—or lack of rewards.

But what if he is no longer around? What if he retired a couple of
years before all these things came together to throw the company into
a tailspin? In that case, he can cry all the way to the bank. Not only did
he receive huge bonuses while he was milking the company, but his

legend is enhanced. After all, profits were booming when he was running the company, but they fell apart right after he left. Superficially it might well appear that the profits boomed *because* he was there and then fell apart *because* he was no longer there. Our hypothetical president may even be called out of retirement to save the company he ruined.

So, in these days of sophisticated technology, international markets, and economies of scale, executives must have the incentive not just to maximize the current year's profits but to take costly actions now to preserve the company's future viability.

This chapter focuses on four long-term incentive devices that share a common premise. The premise is that the market value of a company's stock mirrors long-term performance. Thus if executives make the right decisions now, and if years hence those decisions produce the right results, profits will exhibit excellent growth and in turn will trigger a greatly increased market price for the company's shares. The four long-term incentive devices are qualified stock options, nonqualified stock options, phantom stock, and stock appreciation rights.

Qualified Stock Options

A qualified stock option plan is one which qualifies for favorable tax treatment, provided that certain conditions are met:

- The plan must be approved by the shareholders, and the total number of shares reserved for options over the life of the plan must be specified.
- The plan must expire no later than ten years after it is adopted.
- The option price per share must be at least equal to the fair market value of the stock as of the date any grant is made.
- An individual option must be exercised within five years from its date of grant.
- The optionee must be an employee of the company and, after the grant has been made, may not own more than 5 percent of the total shares outstanding. (This rule has been somewhat liberalized for very small companies.)
- The optionee may not exercise an option so long as another qualified option granted on an earlier date and carrying a higher option price per share is currently outstanding.

Provided that an option meets all these conditions (and a few minor conditions as well) and provided that the executive holds his stock for at least three years after its exercise, he will, when he eventually sells the shares, qualify for long-term capital gains tax treatment on all appreciation which has occurred above the original option price.

The option "spread." For discussion, it is helpful to divide the total appreciation that may occur in an option transaction into two parts. The first is the difference between the option price and the market value of the stock as of the date of exercise. The spread (as this part is called) is what makes an option worthwhile, for it represents risk-free appreciation and an effective discount in the price of the stock that is not available to the ordinary investor. The second portion of appreciation is the gain in the stock's market value that occurs after the option has been exercised but prior to its sale. This portion represents no special advantage for the optionee, for he could obtain it as an ordinary investor simply by purchasing the stock on the open market on the date of exercise.

Tax Consequences to Executives

The Tax Reform Act of 1976 has doomed the qualified stock option. Options granted under plans adopted after May 20, 1976, may no longer be considered qualified. Options granted after May 20, 1976, under plans adopted before that date may be considered qualified if they are exercised within five years of that date—making the maximum exercise period less than five years and thereby diminishing the appeal of the option. Only options granted before May 20, 1976, continue to have all the now-dubious attributes of qualified options.

However, *all* qualified options are subject to potentially stringent taxes under the Tax Reform Act of 1976. To demonstrate let us look first at an executive who holds his stock for at least three years after exercise and then at an executive who sells his stock before the three-year holding period has run out.

In the year he exercises a qualified stock option, the executive's option spread becomes an item of so-called tax preference income. Tax preference income has two unwelcome implications, and to illustrate them, let us assume the executive's spread is $100,000.

First, every dollar of tax preference income wipes out a dollar of personal service income and causes that dollar to be taxed at nonpersonal service income rates. Suppose our hypothetical executive had $300,000 of taxable income stemming from salary and bonus payments. Had he not exercised his qualified stock option, the last $100,000 of this $300,000 would have been taxed at a 50 percent rate, since it would have qualified as personal service income. Now, however, his $100,000 option spread reduces his taxable personal service income from $300,000 to $200,000 and subjects the last $100,000 to taxes at nonpersonal service income rates. In this case, the rate is 70 percent, thus raising the tax bill by $20,000. Note that this tax increase does nothing to the cost basis of his option; hence it is not recoverable in the event that the executive later sells his option stock at no gain, or at a loss.

Second, the executive may be subject to a 15 percent "minimum" tax. To determine this tax he deducts from his $100,000 option spread the greater of two numbers: (1) $10,000 or (2) half his taxes on all his other income. Any amount left over is subject to a flat tax of 15 percent, and this tax too has no effect on the cost basis of the stock and hence is not recoverable.

In general, an executive is not likely to be hit by both these tax consequences. If he has a lot of personal service income, he will have some of it wiped out and taxed at a higher rate. But if he has a lot of personal service income, he also has to pay a lot of taxes on it as well as on his other income. Even half those taxes will probably exceed $10,000 and may exceed the entire option spread, thereby eliminating the 15 percent minimum tax.

However, an executive with a huge personal service income *and* a huge option spread could certainly be hit twice. Suppose for example that the option spread were not $100,000 but $1 million. In that case, *all* of the executive's personal service income would be wiped out, and even after he deducted half his taxes from his $1 million spread, he would still have a large amount left to be taxed at 15 percent.

Once the executive has weathered the tax consequences in the year of option exercise, he can relax until he sells his option stock. Let us assume here that he doesn't sell his stock for at least three years. In that case, his total gain (the value of the stock on the date of the sale minus the price he paid for it) is taxed as a long-term capital gain. To illustrate, let us assume that the total gain at the time of sale is $200,000. First, the executive splits the gain into two equal pieces of $100,000 each. One piece is added to his ordinary nonpersonal service income and is taxed as follows.

1. The first $25,000 is taxed at the lesser of either 50 percent or the regular rates he would pay on an additional $25,000 of nonpersonal service income.

2. The remaining $75,000 is taxed at the regular rates he would pay on an additional $75,000 of nonpersonal service income.

In our example the executive was already in the 70 percent marginal tax bracket for additional nonpersonal service income. He will therefore pay a 50 percent tax on the first $25,000 of this first half of his $200,000 total gain and an additional 70 percent tax on the remaining $75,000, for a total tax of $65,000. This represents 32.5 percent of his total gain of $200,000.

After getting hit by one or both tax consequences in the year he exercised his qualified stock option and then paying a long-term capital gains tax at the time of option sale, the executive may think he is finished. But he isn't. He forgot about the second half of his $200,000 total gain. This half once again becomes an item of tax preference income. And once again it has the effect of wiping out $100,000 of his personal service income and may also be partially subject to the 15 percent minimum tax.

Of course, the executive might decide to sell his option stock before the three years are up, and in that case the tax consequences are different.

If the executive sells his stock in the tax year in which he exercised the option he escapes the penalties associated with tax preference income because he is deemed not to have any tax preference income. However, he is taxed in one of two ways.

1. If the stock has the same or a lower value on the date of sale compared to the date of exercise, the amount by which its value on the date of sale exceeds his purchase price is taxed at personal service income rates—that is, at a maximum of 50 percent.

2. If the stock has a higher value on the date of sale than it did on the date of exercise, the gain is divided into two pieces. The first piece is the amount by which the value of the stock on the date of exercise exceeds the purchase price; this is taxed as personal service income. The second piece is the amount by which the value of the stock on the date of sale exceeds its value on the date of exercise; this is considered a short-term capital gain. If this is the only capital transaction for that year, it is taxed at nonpersonal service income rates as high as 70 percent.

Suppose the executive does not hold his stock for three or more years and does not sell it in the tax year in which he exercised his qualified stock option. Suppose instead he sells his stock during some intervening period. In that case, he is out of luck. Because of the tax preference income rules, any taxes he may have paid in the year of exercise are unrecoverable. Thereafter, the tax consequences are as described, except in the event that the executive has held his stock long enough to qualify for a long-term instead of a short-term capital gain on any appreciation above the value of the stock on the date of exercise. Starting in 1978, the holding period for long-term capital gains is one year.

Tax Consequences to Company

If the executive holds his stock for the required three or more years, the company is not entitled to any tax deduction whatsoever.

However, if the executive sells his stock earlier, in the year the stock is sold the company receives a tax deduction equal to the amount declared by the executive as ordinary income and taxed at personal service income rates.

Accounting Consequences

Under Opinion 25 of the Accounting Principles Board (the predecessor of the Financial Accounting Standards Board), a company utilizing its stock in a compensation plan must charge its pretax earnings by the amount by which the stock's quoted market price on the measurement date exceeds the amount, if any, that the employee must pay for it. The opinion goes on to state that the measurement date is the first date on which two facts are known: (1) the number of shares that an individual employee is entitled to receive and (2) the purchase price, if any.

In analyzing this rule, let us assume that on January 1, 1977, an executive is granted a qualified stock option for 1,000 shares at $100 per share. First we have to determine the measurement date. It turns out to be the date of grant, because that is the first date on which we know both the number of shares that may be purchased (1,000) and the purchase price per share ($100). Next we have to determine the quoted market value of the stock on the measurement date. This turns out to be $100 per share, since a qualified stock option cannot carry an option price lower than the fair market value of the stock on the date of grant. (It could carry a higher price but almost never does.)

Now we are in a position to determine the charge to pretax earnings. That consists of the amount by which the quoted market value of the stock on the measurement date ($100,000, or 1,000 shares times $100) exceeds the purchase price to be paid by the executive ($100,000, or 1,000 shares times $100). Since the difference is zero, there is no charge to the pretax earnings.

This rather creative accounting treatment has led many people to assume, wrongly, that with qualfiied stock options the executive could receive great reward, yet the company would not have to incur a cost. That is true as far as we have gone, but we haven't gone far enough. There *is* a cost, and it shows up in dilution rather than as a charge to earnings.

During the interval between the date of option grant and the date of option exercise, the company may have to increase the number of shares outstanding in figuring earnings per share. The increase will always be less than the 1,000 shares granted, but there *will* be an increase so long as the stock has appreciated above its $100 per share option price. In making this calculation, the company follows the treasury share method of accounting described earlier.

Assuming the option is finally exercised, the company must add the full 1,000 shares to its share base. However, this overstates the dilution that has actually occurred, because the company did receive some consideration from the executive for issuing the shares. To illustrate, let us assume that the shares have appreciated from $100 to $200 apiece by the date of exercise. In this case, the executive gives the company a check for $100,000, and the company in turn issues the 1,000 shares. If the company has no need for this additional capital it can turn right around and buy 500 of its shares on the open market, using the $100,000 to cover the purchase. The company will then have no additional capital, but it will have issued 500 shares for which it implicitly received no consideration (the consideration having been used to buy back the other 500 shares). It is these shares, then, that represent the true cost of the option. For as long as the company stays in business, earnings per share will be diluted by the 500 extra shares issued in connection with the option.

So the maxim that there's no such thing as a free lunch applies even to the world of compensation. The company can give an executive a $100,000 bonus, charge it all off to earnings in a single year, and be done with it. Or it can give the executive $100,000 by means of a stock option transaction, avoid any charges to its earnings, but pay small amounts forever. To put it another way, if you go to Europe you can pay the bill all at once or you can pay $5 per month for 20 years. But you can't go to Europe for nothing.

Or at least that's the way it seems at first glance. But what if you are the CEO of a company? You can give an executive a $100,000 bonus and incur the costs all at once. Or you can pay little by little through the option route—*as long as you are still with the company*. After you leave, the cost continues. But that's not your problem, is it? And before you leave, earnings per share are still higher than they would have been had you elected to pay the bonus and get it over with at once. What would you rather do?

Qualified Stock Options: RIP

Hemlines go up. Hemlines go down. Nothing stays the same forever. And this generalization applies to the world of executive compensation. Qualified stock options were once the most popular of all executive compensation devices; now they have been given the last rites by Congress. It may be instructive to see what happened to bring qualified stock options to such an inglorious end.

First we had the government in the incentive business. Prior to 1964 the maximum marginal tax rate for ordinary income was a whopping 91 percent, whereas the maximum tax rate on a long-term capital gain was only 25 percent. During that same time frame a stock option price could be as low as 85 percent of the fair market value on the date of grant, the option could be exercised over a period as long as ten years, and, most important, it qualified for long-term capital gains tax treatment six months after exercise. Small wonder that companies moved away from cash bonuses and into stock options; the government offered them the incentive to do so.

In 1964 the government decided that it had gone too far. It stipulated that the minimum option price had to be 100 percent of the fair market value of the stock on the date of grant, it shortened the maximum exercise period from ten years to five years, and it lengthened the holding period from six months to three years. At the same time, the maximum tax on ordinary income was lowered from 91 percent to 70 percent. Still, the executive might have a 45 point tax advantage through a qualified stock option, inasmuch as the maximum tax on a long-term capital gain remained steady at 25 percent.

In 1969 the government really began to get tough. First, it made the long-term capital gains tax progressive. From then on the marginal tax could rise as high as 35 percent of the total gain (or, more correctly, 70 percent of half the gain). Second, it introduced the concept of tax preference income, as we have seen. Third, it created a class of personal service income and subjected it to a maximum tax of 50 percent.

Under the Tax Reform Act of 1969 the executive no longer faced a single 25 percent tax consequence on his qualified stock option transaction. If everything went wrong, he faced as many as 13 tax consequences stretching over as many as 10 tax years, and his effective tax rate on his option transaction could rise well above the 50 percent tax he would have paid on an equivalent bonus.

At the same time, the company stood to lose its tax deduction if the executive held his stock for more than three years. Where before, the company gladly forfeited its tax deduction to let the executive reap as much as a 66 point tax advantage prior to 1964 or as much as a 45 point tax advantage between 1964 and 1969, now such behavior no longer made any sense.

In 1976, the government imposed even more onerous tax regulations on the qualified stock option and then prohibited its use after 1981. But such action was superfluous. From a tax standpoint the qualified stock option died in 1969. The 1976 law drove a stake through its heart.

So much for taxes. What about accounting considerations? Clearly, accountants also were in the incentive business. They required a company to pay all at once for a cash bonus, but they let the company use an infinite installment plan in the case of a qualified stock option. Well, accountants are still in the incentive business, but as Eastern Airlines advertises: "You gotta believe!" You gotta believe that the market price of a stock really mirrors the company's long-term peformance. Perhaps it does over a span of decades, but how about a shorter period? The chairman of the People's Republic of China probably has more influence on the price/earnings multiple of an American company's stock than the company's own chairman does. Suddenly stock prices became quite volatile. An increase in earnings per share might be followed by a decrease in the market value of the stock.

Companies began to discover that stock options were perverse. They created a generation of millionaires every so often. But if you didn't hit it right, you made nothing. You may have received an option at the wrong price. Or you may have received one at the right price and exercised it at the wrong price. Or you may have received one at the right price and exercised it at the right price only to sell it at the wrong price—or not sell it at all and see your investment wither.

So downside risk—once a term discussed only by economists—became a reality. And that downside risk was compounded by the burden of financing the option. Until 1964 an executive who wanted to finance a qualified stock option with an aggregate purchase price of $100,000 could borrow the money at about 5 percent interest, then hold the stock for six months to qualify for long-term capital gains tax treatment. Therefore, his interest bill was only $2,500. What's more, he could deduct this interest on his tax return, and if he was at the maximum 91 percent tax bracket, the government would pick up 91 percent of the cost. That left him out of pocket only 9 percent of $2,500, or $225.

The executive who came the same route along about 1973 or so would have discovered that interest rates had risen to 12 percent. His interest costs on a $100,000 loan would be $12,000 per year, and since he had to hold his stock for three years to qualify for long-term capital gains tax treatment, his total interest costs would be $36,000. Ironically, and somewhat perversely, tax rates on ordinary income had fallen from 91 percent to 50 percent. Hence the executive would have found the government willing to pick up only 50 percent of his interest bill through tax deductions. His net cost would have dropped from $36,000 to $18,000, but $18,000 was a neat 80 times the $225 net interest that his predecessor incurred some ten years earlier.

Any one of these factors—tax rates, cost-effectiveness, stock market volatility, and soaring costs of borrowing—would have been enough to finish the qualified stock option. Put them all together and they don't spell M-O-T-H-E-R; they spell R-E-S-T I-N P-E-A-C-E.

Nonqualified Stock Options

If we can't live forever, we can at least gain a semblance of immortality through our children. The child and legitimate heir of the qualified stock option is the nonqualified stock option.

A nonqualified option is one that cannot be qualified. That is to say, it contains a defect that renders it ineligible for qualification under the tax laws. So, instead of setting the option price at not less than 100 percent of the fair market value on the date of grant, the company may set the option price at, say, 50 percent of the fair market value. Or, instead of imposing a maximum exercise period of five years, the company may impose one of ten years. Or, instead of

forbidding exercise of one option as long as another is outstanding
that was granted earlier at a higher price, the company may permit
the option to be exercised at will. Or, instead of doing just one of
these things, the company may do all of them at once.

Tax Consequences

For the executive, in the year of exercise he is required to take
the option spread into his ordinary income. Such income is generally
considered personal service income and is subject to tax at the maximum 50 percent rate. After paying this tax, the executive's cost basis
in the stock is increased from its value at the date of option grant to its
value at the date of option exercise. Thereafter, the executive is
treated like any ordinary investor. If he sells the stock before the end
of the one-year holding period required for long-term capital gains
tax treatment, any gain in the shares above the price prevailing on the
date of option exercise will be a short-term capital gain, and any loss
will be a short-term capital loss. If he holds the stock past the required
date, any gain or loss becomes a long-term capital loss. If he holds the
stock past the required date, any gain or loss becomes a long-term
capital gain or loss.

As for the company, in the year the executive exercises his nonqualified stock option, the company receives a tax deduction equal to
the option spread.

Accounting Consequences

If the option is not discounted—that is, if the option price is at
least equal to the fair market value of the stock on the date of option
grant—there is no charge to pretax earnings. In effect the option is
treated just like a qualified stock option, in that the difference between the quoted market value on the measurement date and the
option price to be paid by the executive is zero.

However, the nonqualified stock option, like the qualified stock
option that is sold before the end of three years, gives the company a
tax deduction. This deduction is not reflected in reported earnings
but instead bypasses the income statement and goes directly into capital surplus. The reason, as was seen earlier, is that the effect of a tax
deduction can be shown in reported earnings only to the extent that a
commensurate charge has been taken to reported earnings. Since no
charge was taken, no tax deduction shows up either. To balance out

the fact that the company is actually paying less in taxes than is shown in the annual report, a sideline contribution is made to capital surplus.

If the nonqualified stock option is discounted—that is, if the option price is less than the fair market value of the stock on the date of option grant—the amount of the discount at the time of grant must be charged to pretax earnings. This charge is apportioned ratably to each year between the date of grant and the end of the option exercise period, notwithstanding that the option is exercised earlier, is exercised for a gain that is less than the discount, or is not exercised at all.

To illustrate the accounting treatment, let us assume that an executive is granted a 1,000 share option at $50 per share when the fair market value is $100 per share. Since the number of shares that may be exercised and the purchase price are known at the time of option grant, that date becomes the measurement date. The quoted market value of the shares on that date is $100,000 (1,000 shares times $100 each), but the purchase price to be paid by the executive is only $50,000 (1,000 shares times $50 each). The difference—$50,000—must be charged to pretax earnings, but not all at once. If, for example, the option may be exercised during a ten-year period, a charge of $5,000 will be made each year for ten years.

Since a charge is being made to earnings, the company is allowed to reflect a commensurate tax deduction. Assuming a $5,000 charge to pretax earnings and a 48 percent marginal tax rate, the company is permitted to lower its reported provision for federal income taxes by $2,400. This in turn causes reported aftertax profits to decline by the difference between $5,000 and $2,400, or $2,600. As we have seen, this reduced provision for federal income taxes shows up at the same time as the charge to pretax earnings itself, even though the company must wait until the executive actually exercises his option to obtain its tax deduction.

Note that the company is permitted to reduce its reported provision for federal income taxes only to the extent of the charge to pretax earnings. If the executive later exercises his option when the fair market value has appreciated beyond the value at the time of the grant, the extra tax deduction given to the company cannot be shown in reported earnings, because such appreciation was not charged to earnings. The effect of this extra tax deduction goes directly into capital surplus, as is the case for an undiscounted, nonqualified stock option.

Typical Terms

Although companies are permitted to offer a nonqualified option at a discount, few of them do so. Discounted options attract vigorous shareholder opposition, and besides, the discount must be charged against earnings no matter what happens later. Perhaps the option will never be exercised. Or perhaps profits will plummet during some future year. No matter. The company will still be stuck with the charge to earnings.

What most companies do is to grant an undiscounted option and then allow ten years in which to exercise it. Given the volatility of the stock market, it is obvious that a longer option period offers the executive a better chance to ride out the ups and downs of the market and perhaps earn something out of his option grant.

It is noteworthy that the typical terms of a nonqualified option— no discount and a ten-year exercise period—were at least to some extent influenced by SEC rules governing insider trading. Until recently, SEC considered the grant of a stock option to be an exempt transaction (neither a purchase nor a sale) only if the option was not discounted and carried a term of no more than ten years. Now the rules have been changed, and the grant of any option, whether discounted or not and whether granted for a period of more or less than ten years, is considered an exempt transaction. Probably, the use of discounting will remain restricted, notwithstanding the liberalized SEC stance, because of the other reasons already mentioned. But companies may quite possibly begin to extend the exercise period for nonqualified stock options beyond ten years.

Advantages of Nonqualified Options

Compared to the qualified stock option, the nonqualified option has a lot going for it—at least for the moment.

First, it is a fairly flexible compensation device. It can be discounted. It can be offered with a very long exercise period. It can be exercised in any order.

Second, it is a relatively unobtrusive form of compensation. Charges to earnings can be avoided if the option is not discounted. What's more, it will show up in the proxy statement in a less forceful way than an equivalent amount of cash bonus.

Third, it is subject to tax at the maximum 50 percent rate—a rate that is relatively low compared not only to past U.S. tax trends but also to current tax trends in many other countries.

Fourth, it is cost-effective to the company. The amount of true dilution occasioned by a nonqualified stock option is less than that of a qualified stock option, because the company receives consideration not only from the executive but, in a manner of speaking, from the government as well. So, if the company does want to use additional capital to buy back shares from the open market after an option has been exercised, it can use not only the monies paid by the executive but the tax savings contributed by the government as a result of the option's deductibility.

Fifth, the executive has lessened borrowing costs. If he is not an officer or director of his company, and if the shares are registered, and if the company isn't upset by sales of option stock, he can turn his option into cash on the day he exercises it. If he is an officer he will have to hold his shares for six months, but that is far less than the three years required for qualified options.

Finally, options of any sort remain prime executive status symbols. The fact that the executive receives one is sometimes as important as whether he makes any money from it.

Of course, the nonqualified stock option is subject to the vicissitudes of the market price. If the market price of a company's stock does not in fact mirror long-term achievements, then from a motivational standpoint an option is essentially worthless.

Administrative Aspects of Stock Options

Before moving on to phantom stock grants and stock appreciation rights, let us look at the ways various companies administer their option plans.

Provisions imposed by the company. Stock option plans often contain additional provisions imposed, not as a matter of law, but by the company. For example, a given option grant may not be exercised immediately; 25 percent of the total number of shares can be exercised (on a cumulative basis) on each of the first four anniversaries succeeding the date of the grant. Such features are known as delayed exercise provisions.

Eligibility

The size of the stock option eligible group varies widely—and wildly—among companies. Some companies give virtually every employee an option—even the janitors. On the other end of the spectrum, the eligible group may consist of only five to ten top executives. Part of the reason for this wide variance is the great secrecy with which companies typically surround their stock option plans. Although companies exchange base salary and bonus information quite freely, for some reason they are loath to talk about their option plans.

Statistically speaking, however, the average company includes far fewer executives for stock option eligibility than for bonus eligibility. In one study of 13 large companies, the smallest of which had 30,000 employees, the average number of eligibles was 236, and the average percentage of total population covered for eligibility was 0.3 percent. In the same group of companies, bonus eligibility, on the other hand, typically averaged one percent of total population.

Size of Grants

The relationship between the size of stock option grants and base salary is similar to the relationship between bonuses and base salary described earlier. In effect, as the salary rises, the size of the grant rises even faster. This is illustrated in Figure 3.

In this exhibit, stock option grants during a five-year period have been converted into a multiple of base salary and then related to the executive's base salary. To illustrate, suppose an executive whose salary was $100,000 received one option during a five-year period consisting of 4,000 shares at an option price of $50 per share. The size of his option as a multiple of his base salary was 2.0 ($200,000 divided by $100,000). If the executive had received not one but several options during the five-year period under study, the separate options would have been added together and the resulting figure divided by the ending base salary to establish the multiple.

It can be seen from this exhibit that the option multiple increases as the salary increases. Thus an individual with a base salary of $30,000 per year is, on the average, likely to receive an amount equal to his salary—or $30,000—in option stock during a five-year period. On the other hand, an executive with a base salary of $200,000 is, on the average, likely to receive four times his salary—or $800,000—in option stock during a five-year period.

As with option eligibility, option sizes vary greatly around the average. Thus individual multiples making up the average that equals salary at the $30,000 level ranged from 0.3 to 3.5 times base salary. Similarly, the multiples making up the average of 4 times salary at the $200,000 salary level ranged from 2.1 to 12 times salary.

Figure 3. Option multiples versus base salary.

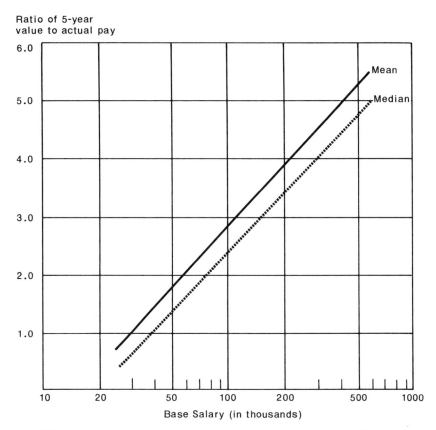

Ratio of 5-year
value to actual pay

Base Salary (in thousands)

The size of stock options is therefore quite considerable—especially at the higher salary levels. Size, however, does not necessarily translate into income for the optionee—even $1 million of option stock will be worthless if the market price stays the same or declines. Nevertheless, the size of the grant defines the opportunity for appreciation and is therefore of considerable importance.

Frequency of Grants

Stock option grants, unlike base salary payments and bonus awards, are not necessarily made each year. Until recently, in fact, the usual practice was to make large grants at infrequent intervals—for example, once every five years.

More frequent—usually annual—grants are being used more often, and for good reasons. First, an annual grant permits dollar averaging of option prices.

A large grant of option stock at what later turns out to be a spuriously high option price can effectively exclude an individual from the plan for up to five years. With smaller grants, the individual is at least given the opportunity to get a more appetizing but later grant.

Second, the use of annual option grants allows a better balance between grants and performance. (It sometimes happens that an individual who receives a large grant fails to live up to his initial promise.) Annual grants also give the executive the feeling that the company hasn't forgotten him—the "what have you done for me lately?" syndrome.

When coupled with delayed exercise provisions, annual grants also offer a degree of holding power, and on a less negatively oriented basis than the golden handcuffs approach used in bonus plans. For example, suppose a company combines annual grants with a provision that makes 50 percent of the option exercisable on the first anniversary of the grant and the second 50 percent (plus any portion of the first 50 percent not yet exercised) on the second anniversary of the grant. With this approach, no more than 70 percent of an executive's option stock will be exercisable at any given point in time; and 30 percent of his stock will be subject to forfeiture in the event of his termination. (Of five consecutive annual grants, all equal in size, three will be fully exercisable, one will be 50 percent exercisable, and the most recent will not be exercisable; hence the 70 percent figure just mentioned.) Unlike the golden handcuffs approach in bonus awards, the executive is not faced with giving up something he has already gained, but with losing something he never had in the first place.

Smaller, more frequent option grants also seem to be preferred by individual executives.

Granting Guidelines

Too often, decisions regarding option grants are extremely casual. When the president thinks about it (perhaps when he himself has run out of option stock), he will consider making additional grants to his subordinates. After a hurried and superficial performance assessment, grants are made, usually involving multiples of 500 shares—which, after all, are nice even numbers. Of course, if the stock happens to be priced in the IBM range, a mistake of 500 shares could result in an error of about $150,000.

A better approach is to establish annual granting multiples for various salary levels. For example, suppose that a company links the midpoints of its salary ranges to competitive going rates of base salary and that one of those ranges has a midpoint of $50,000. Using the survey data from Figure 3 or from some similar survey, the company discovers that a competitive five-year option granting multiple at the $50,000 salary level is 1.8 times salary. Dividing this figure by five because it wishes to make grants annually, the company comes up with a multiple of 0.36 times salary. This figure is then applied to the $50,000 base salary midpoint and divided by the current market value per share of the company's stock to obtain a guideline number of option shares for that particular year's grant. Assuming that the stock is then selling for $100 per share, the guideline grant will be 180 shares.

Under certain circumstances the actual grant to a particular executive could vary from the guideline grant. For example, suppose that the current market price is extraordinarily high or low. If it is high the company may want to increase the share grants for that particular year, since the potential for further appreciation is likely to be very low. If the price is low the company may want to decrease share grants to minimize the chances of a windfall to the executives.

At the same time, the company may well want to take the executive's personal performance contributions into account. If his performance is outstanding and gives promise of going on at the same level, why not give him a greater-than-guideline grant? Conversely, if he is resting on his oars, perhaps he should receive a less-than-guideline grant or even no grant at all.

Determining the Number of Option Shares Needed

There is no longer any governmental requirement that an option plan be approved by a company's shareholders. However, unless such a plan is approved, along with the aggregate number of shares that may be issued in connection with the plan, the grant of stock options will not be considered by SEC to be an exempt transaction. This fact, plus a growing uneasiness, has led boards of directors to submit most option plans for shareholder approval. Accordingly it is important to select a total-share figure that will suffice for the life of the plan, but will not be excessive. Two methods may be employed.

The first involves an internal analysis of the company's probable needs. Here the company derives a guideline grant for each eligible and multiplies the various guideline grants by the number of eligibles in each category. It then has to make certain assumptions for future years, including likely escalation in the salaries of current eligibles and in the market price of the stock, as well as in the number of eligibles that may be added. Finally, the company may add shares to arrive at a rounded figure and to provide for certain contingencies.

The company should also examine the share-funding levels in other companies' plans. This can be done on a company-by-company basis, or broad industry survey information (such as was provided by The Conference Board) can be analyzed. The figures produced by the internal and external comparisons should be similar. If they are not, the company may have to take appropriate action with respect to the size of its eligible group, for in those conflict situations that do occur, internal funding needs typically exceed those considered reasonable from an external standpoint, thereby pointing to an inflated eligible group.

Registering the Option Stock

Most companies register their option stock, but some companies look envyingly at those that do not. Unregistered option stock requires an investment representation from the optionee before it can be exercised. This representation prevents the executive from selling his option stock except at a substantial discount for a period of two years.

Thus we have a seemingly ingenious way of forcing executives to hold on to their option stock. However, the use of unregistered stock is another negatively oriented motivational device that may be bitterly resented by the company's optionees. And, since few companies use unregistered stock, the company's plan is automatically made less competitive.

Therefore, the use of unregistered shares is counterproductive. The costs of registration are not very high in absolute terms, and they are dirt cheap in relation to the costs of the stock option plan itself.

The Pressure to Hold

As implied, the use of unregistered shares is symptomatic of a larger problem: the desire of top management to have optionees hang on to their option stock.

There are two basic conflicts. The first is between the company and its shareholders and gets the company hung up on its own rhetoric. In most companies, the stock option plan is touted to the shareholders as a means whereby the executives, through stock ownership, will share the same personal objectives as the shareholders themselves. On the other hand, the company also knows that in practice the stock option is a well-deserved form of executive compensation. An executive who sells his option shares therefore goes against the expressed purpose of the stock option plan. And shareholders have been known to become quite displeased when a pattern of frequent "dumping" occurs. One valid reason for their anger is that issuance of new shares to fund an option plan (which is the usual practice) dilutes the holdings of the remaining shareholders. If these people are to have their equity diluted and lose the supposed motivational advantages of the plan to boot as a result of option stock sales, they have every reason to be angry.

The second conflict involves the individual optionee. He is given a huge grant of stock, which he may have considerable difficulty in financing, and is then expected to hold his shares no matter what. If he sells, he may receive a midnight phone call from the president, be passed over for promotion, or worse. As long as the stock rises meteorically, few problems are likely. But if the stock drops meteorically, the executive is caught in a crunch between company loyalty and his own pocketbook.

It makes no motivational sense—and indeed is cruel—to offer candy to a baby and then slap the hand that reaches out. Just so, it makes no motivational sense—and indeed is cruel—to offer an executive a large option, or even a series of smaller options, and then insist that they be held in all circumstances. The company that cannot bear to see its executives sell their shares should refrain from using stock in its executive compensation package.

Terminating the Option

IRS regulations state that a qualified stock option must expire no later than 90 days after termination of employment for reasons other than death and no later than one year after death. Most companies simply adopt the IRS language in designing their own plans—even nonqualified option plans.

Options should expire on the date of termination, however, if the individual is quitting voluntarily or is being discharged for cause.

Allowing options for these people to continue for another 90 days simply gives them a free ride on any further appreciation. Considering the reasons for the terminations, such an approach makes no sense at all.

Allowing the 90-day post-termination period for cases of retirement, disability, and such is of course a sound procedure.

Company Loans

A few companies, but a very few, offer their executives company loans to finance the purchase of option shares. Occasionally such loans are interest-free; but more often than not, some interest is payable, even though the rate may be nominal compared to what the executive would pay to a bank.

A company loan may be appealing to the executive, but it is fraught with problems for the company. First, the laws of certain states prohibit loans to senior executives or limit the amounts that may be lent. Second, the company must generally conform with the margin requirements imposed by the Federal Reserve Board, and thus the amount of the loan may be limited from this standpoint as well. Third, loans are messy transactions and could involve a conflict of interest when made to senior executives. They create the appearance if not the fact of self-dealing, especially if the interest rate is quite low compared to the going bank rate. Fourth, many shareholders become incensed when they read about loans to executives—and so do rank-and-file employees who are denied similar loan privileges. Finally, if the executive defaults the company may be placed in the position of having to go to court to recover its money. Not only is this expensive, it is also embarrassing.

These problems make most companies steer clear of loans to executives. If a company is willing to put in a friendly word with its lead bank about a favored executive, the bank may then decide to grant a loan. But the company is not a signatory to such a loan, and in the event of a default the company incurs no liability.

Option Swaps

Whenever an option sinks substantially underwater—that is, when the market price of the stock is significantly below the option price—the subject of option swaps comes up. In effect, should the company offer the executive the opportunity to turn in his old option and receive a new one, for the same or a lesser number of shares, at the current low market price?

Some companies simply do nothing until it is time to make the next normal option grant. If the executive realizes nothing from his earlier underwater grant, so be it. This approach certainly has merit in a system featuring small annual grants, since no single underwater option is likely to be large enough to cause any major problem, and the next grant will be made in a matter of months. But the company that adopts this posture in the face of huge grants made only once every five years may find that the executive won't tolerate such treatment. Why should he when he can quit, join the company across the street, and receive a similar option that is not underwater?

If the company has plenty of shares left in its option plan, it can ignore the underwater option and give the executive a new grant—one that supplements his underwater grant and his next normal grant. This avoids the problems associated with an option swap, and it creates no real problems as long as the underwater option is worthless. But what if the market surges? In that case the executive will reap a windfall, because he will have been granted too many shares.

When all else fails, the company can consider an actual option swap. But it had better brace itself for severe shareholder criticism. After all, a shareholder who buys his shares at $50 each cannot make any profit unless the shares rise above $50 in value. But if an executive receives an option at $50, then the stock plummets to $25, then the option is swapped for a new one carrying an option price of $25, and then the stock rises to $35, he will make a decent profit.

In fact, option swapping came to be such an emotional topic that the New York Stock Exchange now requires explicit shareholder approval before listed companies make any swaps.

Option swapping should be avoided wherever possible, and in most cases it can be avoided by a system of smaller annual option grants. If it must be done, a reasonable way to do it is to invoke a penalty, requiring the executive to forfeit more shares at the underwater price for fewer shares at the current price. It might also make sense to have the new option expire on the date when the old, canceled option would have expired rather than allowing the new option to carry a full exercise period.

Phantom Stock Grants

A few companies have sought to eliminate the financing problems associated with stock options by making so-called phantom stock grants. This entails granting the executive not shares but units. Generally, the initial price of each unit is equal to the market price of a share of stock on the date the unit is granted. The final price of each unit is equal to the market price of a share of stock at some future date, usually five years later. When the final price has been determined, the excess of the final price over the initial price, if any, is paid to the executive in cash or in an equivalent number of free shares.

Under this approach the executive need incur no financing costs and no downside risk. He just sits back, enjoys the ride, and at the end receives a fat check which can immediately be spent on the little things that make life worthwhile—yachts, for instance.

Or does he? What if the market price rises smartly during the first four years of the grant and then plummets in the fifth year? If the executive had been granted a regular stock option, and if he had been sagacious enough to exercise his option at the end of the fourth year (which he will tell you he is sagacious enough to have done), he would have reaped a substantial profit. Now he gets nothing. So a phantom stock grant may be great under certain conditions and terrible under others.

For its part, the company doesn't have much of a deal either. Since the company is essentially paying the executive a bonus—one that happens to be tied to market appreciation, but a bonus nevertheless—it must charge its pretax earnings with whatever it pays. Any charge to earnings gives some companies pause, but this charge has a nasty little twist because its size cannot be anticipated. The company can mitigate the charge by taking accruals during the five-year period, and indeed it must do so according to the accounting rules. But what if the stock booms in the last quarter of the fifth year? At that point, the charge may mushroom and do severe damage to the company's profit and loss statement.

Remember, too, that the charge to earnings, besides being unpredictable and uncontrollable, may bear no relation to the company's underlying earnings. Thus the increase in the market price of the stock may not have stemmed from an increase in earnings per share but rather from an increase in the market value of stocks generally.

Phantom stock has a lot of glitter, but touch it too long and your fingers may turn green!

Stock Appreciation Rights

A stock appreciation right (SAR) is an accessory that an increasing number of companies have been hanging on their nonqualified stock options. With SARs attached the executive has the privilege of turning in any or all of his option shares, so long as they are exercisable at the time, and receiving a payment equal to the amount by which the then current value of such shares exceeds their option price. The payment can be made in cash or in an equivalent number of free shares of stock.

To illustrate, let us assume that an executive is granted 1,000 nonqualified option shares at an option price of $100 per share and that each share has an SAR attached. Let us also assume that the shares rise in value to $200 each during the exercise period of the option. At that point, the executive has the choice of exercising his option shares or turning them in to take advantage of the SARs. If he chooses the SAR route, he forfeits his 1,000 option shares and receives an immediate economic benefit of $100,000, the spread in his option shares. This benefit may be satisfied by paying him $100,000 in cash, by issuing him 500 free shares each of which is worth $200, or by some combination of these methods, such as $50,000 in cash plus 250 free shares. (Some companies leave the form of payment up to the executive; others permit the executive to express a preference, while reserving the final decision to themselves; still others take a rigid, no-choice posture.)

Thus, an SAR is rather like a floating phantom stock grant—floating in the sense that the executive can choose, within broad limits, the time he wishes to receive his stock gain. Unlike a classic phantom stock grant, he does not have to wait until the end of some preestablished period, perhaps only to find that his gain has evaporated.

Payments of SARs, whether in cash or stock, are taxable to the executive at personal service income rates (maximum of 50 percent) when he receives them. Such payments are also deductible to the company in the tax year when they are made.

From an accounting standpoint, all payments of SARs must be charged against pretax earnings. If stock is used to satisfy the payment, the company takes a double-barreled charge against earnings per share—first in the charge against earnings and second in the increase in the number of shares outstanding. In such a case, however, the company does receive additional capital, since it never actually laid out any cash.

A combination nonqualified stock option/SAR plan presents something of an accounting conundrum. If the option is not discounted, and if the executive actually exercises the option instead of grabbing for the SARs, the company sustains no charges to its earnings. But if the executive takes the SAR feature of the plan, the company is required to charge its earnings. How can the company know what to do, except after the fact?

According to Opinion 25, the company must guess as to the action the executive will eventually take and then account for its guess accordingly. If the company assumes the executive will exercise his options, not his SARs, it takes no charge to earnings. If it assumes the executive will take his SARs, it begins to accrue charges to earnings as it would do for a phantom stock plan.

But what if the company guesses wrong? In that case it must rectify the mistake forthwith. If it has not charged earnings because it believed the executive would exercise his option, and in fact the executive exercises his SARs, it must take a charge to earnings (all at once if the SAR is exercised at the end of the option exercise period). If it has accrued charges to earnings because it believed the executive would exercise his SARs, but in fact he exercises his options, the company is permitted to reverse those charges out of earnings. In effect, the company gets to increase its earnings in the year it discovered it had been overaccruing.

In practice, it shouldn't be difficult to guess which way the executive will bounce. As one CEO trenchantly observed: "If one of my executives exercised his options and left his SARs on the table, I'd fire him for stupidity!"

There would appear to be little value in granting SARs to those who are not officers or directors. As noted earlier, if the option shares are registered, and if the company doesn't object to the individual's selling his shares, the optionee can buy and sell his shares in a single day. Perhaps he has to do a bit of running up and down stairs between his office, the treasurer's office, the bank, and the local office of Merrill Lynch, but by the end of the day he has concocted his own do-it-yourself SAR plan. He has his cash and the company has no charge to its earnings.

In the case of officers and directors, however, the grant of SARs in connection with nonqualified stock options can be of real advantage. To illustrate, let us assume that an officer has a 1,000 share nonqualified stock option at an option price of $100 per share and that the market price has appreciated to $200 per share by the time the option is exercised. The company officer has to come up, not with $100,000, but with $150,000 or more to exercise his option. He pays the company $100,000 for his shares, but his $100,000 gain is immediately taxable. Assuming he is at the maximum tax rate of 50 percent for personal service income, he will also have to cough up $50,000 for federal taxes alone (and don't forget about state and local taxes).

All this wouldn't be so bad if the executive could turn around and sell some or all of his shares. But being an insider, he must hold the shares for at least six months to realize any profit. So, during the six-month holding period, he has to incur interest costs.

If he's lucky those are the only costs he'll incur. But suppose the stock, which was worth $200 per share on the date of exercise, begins to plummet during the six-month holding period. At the least, the executive will lose some or all of his gain. (When the stock drops back to $100 per share, he can sell it, notwithstanding that the six-month holding period has not been completed. The reason is that there is no longer any profit between the value of the stock and the price he paid for it.)

Even worse is the fact that he may lose some of the money he paid to the government in taxes. When he gave the government $50,000 to cover the taxes on his $100,000 gain, he automatically stepped up his cost basis in the shares from $100 each to $200 each. When he sells at a price less than $200, he ends up with a short-term capital loss. He may eventually get his $50,000 of taxes back by using his capital loss to offset capital gains and/or writing some of it off against his other ordinary income, but it may be years before he gets it all back.

Thus an SAR, payable in cash, can be of significant help to the corporate officer or director. He doesn't have to borrow anything. He can't lose if the stock plummets during what would otherwise be the six-month holding period. And he can pay his taxes out of the check he receives in satisfaction of the SAR exercise. For its part, the company has to take a charge to earnings for the SAR, and the charge is neither predictable nor controllable. But assuming that the company doesn't have too many officers and makes grants of SARs only to officers, the charge may be relatively manageable.

Prior to the end of 1976, the status of SARs for officers was quite clouded. The Securities and Exchange Commission had blessed the payment of SARs in company stock, because the payment of such shares was deemed to be a purchase, thereby preventing the executive from realizing any profit during the next six months. But the SEC inclination was to view the payment of SARs in cash as a so-called collapsed transaction. In effect, the cash could be viewed as the end result of having exercised the option shares and having immediately sold them for a profit. Clearly, cash received under such circumstances would have to be returned to the company under the insider trading rules.

After further deliberation, however, the SEC conclusion was that a company could pay an officer's SARs in cash, provided that certain rules were observed. The rules are rather detailed, but in many cases they can be met without imposing undue strain on either the executive or the company.

Now that SEC has opened the gates for the settlement of SARs in cash, many more companies are likely to start attaching a shiny new SAR to each option they issue—or at least to each option they issue to those who come within the SEC definition of insiders.

Other
Long-Term
Incentives_____7

We have examined four long-term incentive devices geared to rewarding company executives for an increase in the market value of their company's stock. We have also examined the historical reasons underlying the popularity of market price incentives.

But are such incentives right in today's environment? First, consider the question of taxation. As we have seen, the qualified stock option was the only long-term incentive device that seemingly promised a tax advantage to the executive. But changes in the tax laws have severely eroded the advantage. The qualified stock option was rendered cost-ineffective from a corporate standpoint when the company's tax deduction was lost. In effect, the company had discovered it could give the executive a somewhat larger economic benefit that was taxable at personal service income rates, take its own tax deduction on the benefit, and save money in the process, while putting the same aftertax dollars in the executive's pocket as he had before. Or, if it wished to be really generous, the company could give the executive substantially more aftertax dollars at the same net cost to itself.

When Congress put an end to this moribund compensation device, we were left with the nonqualified stock option, the phantom stock grant, and the stock appreciation right. Compared to the qualified stock option, each of these looked better from a tax standpoint, but each was taxed exactly the same as an equivalent amount of cash —that is, at personal service income rates.

So there is no longer any tax advantage in using the market price of a company's stock as the measuring rod of long-term executive performance.

Why Market Price as Performance Measure?

Which brings us to the bedrock question underlying any compensation plan. Is there any *motivational* advantage to using the market price of a company's stock as the long-term performance measuring rod?

Consider the reply of a board chairman when a dissident stockholder asked what the top executives were doing about "the deplorable market price of our stock." "I hate to answer a question with a question, but in this case I have to. What are *you* doing about the deplorable price of our stock? For our part, the senior executives of this company have doubled the earnings per share over the last five years, improved our return on shareholders' equity, and substantially increased dividends. We simply cannot control the price/earnings multiple. Now, I'm not a trained economist, but I have the feeling that if you and the other shareholders went out and bought some more shares, the market price would go up. So I have to ask what you are doing about the price of our stock. We're doing everything we can."

Perhaps the senior executives can do something about the *relative* price/earnings multiple of their company's stock. But the *absolute* price/earnings multiple, and hence the absolute market value of the shares, is determined by macroeconomic forces which transcend any single company or even any single industry. That being the case, putting all the long-term incentive eggs in the market price basket is not a whole lot different from basing an incentive for executives on the nation's gross national product.

Taking this logic to its conclusion, one could reason that senior executives should have no part of their compensation package riding on the market price of their company's stock. In effect, they should be insulated from the price/earnings multiple, with the shareholders taking all the risk on the multiple—and all the reward too. But perhaps that is too harsh a position. As one CEO put it: "Suppose I receive a huge reward for a steady, long-term improvement in earnings per share, and suppose I receive this reward at the very time the market price of the stock has plummeted to a five-year low. What am I supposed to say to the shareholder who asks about the depressed price of our stock? 'Gee, I didn't realize that our shares had plummeted, because I rarely bother to look up the price of our stock nowadays. But I'm awfully sorry, and I sure hope things turn around soon!' "

Rightly or wrongly, a growing number of companies no longer believe that all long-term incentive rewards should be predicated solely on movements in the market price of their shares. But they do not believe that their rewards should be totally insulated from such movements either. Implicitly, their top managers believe they should be given some incentive to increase the market price of the shares, coupled with an additional incentive to produce solid results over the long term—results like growth in earnings per share that are directly in the shareholders' interests.

In a recent survey more than 80 large companies revealed that they had moved to this newer philosophy, and they represent the leading edge of change. With each round of proxy statements, more and more companies are moving in this direction.

Classic Performance Shares

Let us now examine some of the alternative long-term incentive compensation devices that, alone or in combination with others, operate to give executives some incentive on the market price and on long-term internal results.

An incentive is offered: "Up until now, we granted only nonqualified stock options as our long-term incentive device. Were we to continue this practice, you would be receiving a competitive annual grant of 1,000 nonqualified stock option shares at $100 per share, which is the current market value. However, we have changed plans.

"You are hereby granted the opportunity to earn 500 shares of stock totally free. You will receive these shares five years from now, provided that two conditions are met. First, you must remain with the company during the five-year period. If you should voluntarily resign or be discharged for cause, you will forfeit the opportunity to earn any free shares. Second, cumulative earnings per share during the five-year period must be at least equal to a 10 percent average annual growth in earnings per share.

"This doesn't mean that earnings per share must increase at a steady 10 percent or more in each and every year of the five-year period, but it does mean that this rate of increase must be achieved on average. So you could receive the full payout if earnings per share don't increase at all in one year, provided that they increase by 20 percent or so the following year—or did increase by that amount in the preceding year. If average annual growth in earnings per share is less than 10 percent, the number of free shares you receive will also be less. If the average annual growth in earnings per share is 9 percent, you will receive 400 free shares. If the average annual growth in earnings per share is 8 percent, you will receive 300 free shares. And so on. If average annual growth in earnings per share sinks below 5 percent, you will receive no free shares.

"At the option of the company, payment may be made in cash instead of free shares. Or payment may be made in a combination of cash and free shares."

Tax Consequences

In the year when the executive receives his free shares, their full value is includible in his ordinary income and taxed at personal service income rates (maximum of 50 percent).

In the year when the executive reports income for his free shares, the company receives a tax deduction for a like amount.

Accounting Consequences

Until Opinion 25 was issued a company had to charge its pretax earnings with the product of (1) the number of shares actually earned by the executive at the end of the five-year performance period and (2) the market price of each share at the beginning of the five-year period. Accruals were required during the period.

With Opinion 25 the rules changed. To illustrate, let us assume that our hypothetical executive earns all 500 free shares because the growth in annual earnings per share averaged more than 10 percent during the five-year period. Let us further assume that the market price per share has doubled, from $100 at the beginning of the period to $200 at the end. Recall that the charge to pretax earnings equals the quoted market value on the measurement date less the purchase price, if any, paid by the executive. Recall also that the measurement date is the first date on which we know both the number of shares that may be earned and the purchase price per share.

First we have to ascertain the measurement date. On the date of contingent grant—that is, at the beginning of the period—we know the purchase price per share, which is zero. But we do not know the number of shares that may be earned, because that number is contingent on growth in earnings per share during the period.

The first date on which we know *both* the number of shares that may be earned and the purchase price is the end of the five-year period, which becomes the measurement date. On that date the executive earns 500 shares, each of which has a market value of $200. The quoted market value on the measurement date is therefore $100,000 (500 shares times $200). Since the executive's purchase price is zero, the charge to earnings is accordingly $100,000. Accruals during the five years must be taken. If the company unwittingly overaccrues in one or more years (because the market price later drops, for example, or because growth in earnings per share decreases), the company is entitled to take a credit to earnings in a later year.

Evaluation

Classic performance shares offer two important advantages. First, they mitigate the influence of the market price on the executives' long-term rewards, but they don't eliminate it entirely.

To illustrate let us compare Company A, the company we have been discussing, and Company B, which continues to grant its comparable executive a straight nonqualified stock option for 1,000 shares at $100 per share. Let us go on to assume that both companies manage to increase their earnings per share by an average of 10 percent per year during the five-year performance period.

Now let's assume that the market price per share of both stocks rises from $100 to $200. The executive in Company A receives a pretax economic benefit of $100,000, consisting of 500 free shares worth $200 each. The executive in Company B also receives a pretax economic benefit of $100,000, since that is the amount by which the fair market value of his stock options exceeds the price he must pay to exercise them. At that point our executives come out even.

Now let's assume that the market price of both stocks rises from $100 to $300. The executive in Company A receives a pretax economic benefit of $150,000, consisting of 500 free shares worth $300 each. However, the executive in Company B receives a pretax economic benefit of $200,000.

But what happens if the shares don't increase at all—a not infrequent occurrence these days. In that case the executive in Company A will receive a pretax economic benefit of $50,000 consisting of 500 free shares worth $100 each. His counterpart in Company B will receive nothing, since there has been no appreciation in the stock.

Or suppose the shares decline from $100 to $50. The executive in Company A receives a pretax economic benefit of $25,000, consist-

ing of 500 free shares worth $50 each; obviously the executive in
Company B receives nothing.

What Company A did was to start with a quart jar containing a
100 percent market price incentive. It then poured a goodly amount
of the contents down the drain, but left some in the jar. Finally, it
topped up the jar with an incentive for long-term growth in earnings
per share. Competitively speaking, Company A is offering the same
quart of long-term incentive opportunity as Company B, but a different blending. At a given point, as we have seen, the payoff to both
executives will be the same; at other points the payoffs will be different. If market prices soar the executive in Company B will make more
—a lot more if Company A's earnings per share growth is simultaneously poor. But if there is little growth, no growth, or even negative
growth in the market prices, coupled with good earnings per share
performance in Company A, that company's executive will come out
the winner.

The second advantage of classic performance shares is that they
can lessen or remove financing burdens. The executive in Company B
not only has to pay the tax on his option spread but has to come up
with the purchase price as well. The executive in Company A has no
purchase price; all he has to pay is the taxes on the shares he receives.
And if the payment is made partially or wholly in cash, he is in even
better shape.

From the company standpoint, classic performance shares can
certainly be seen as more motivational than straight nonqualified
stock options. Yet they are troubling from an accounting standpoint.
Not only does the company have to take a charge to earnings, but the
charge is unpredictable and uncontrollable. Because of the change in
accounting rules, classic performance shares have some of the same
disadvantages as phantom stock grants, in that part of the charge to
earnings is predicated on future movements in the market price of
the company's stock.

Modified Performance Shares

Until the accounting rules changed, classic performance shares were
gaining considerable momentum. Now they have outlived their use-
fulness, but they have spawned some healthy children. Let's look at
some of them.

A different incentive is offered: "You are hereby granted 500
nonqualified stock option shares at an option price of $100 each, the

current market value of our stock. The options may not be exercised for five years, then they are exercisable for two years, after which they will expire. You are also hereby granted the opportunity to earn 500 shares free at the end of a five-year period.

"To do so, you must remain with the company during this period. Furthermore, the growth in average earnings per share during the period must equal or exceed 10 percent per year. If it is less, the number of shares you may earn will also be less. Finally, whatever free shares you earn will be delivered only if the market price at the end of the five year period does not exceed $100 per share. If the market price does exceed $100 per share, you will receive a lesser number of shares equal in value to the shares you would have received had the market price been exactly $100 per share.

"To illustrate, assume that our company makes its 10 percent per year earnings per share growth goal and that the share price at the end of the five years is $50, $100, or $200 each. If share prices are $50 or $100 each, you will receive 500 shares free—or an equivalent amount of cash if the company elects this manner of payment. But if the shares are worth $200 each, you will receive only 250 free shares, which will give you the same $50,000 value (250 shares times $200 each) as you would have received from 500 shares at a market price of $100 each.

"Perhaps this feature of our plan will seem unfair, since you seem to derive no benefit from any increase in the market price above $100. But remember you also have a nonqualified option. To benefit from that market price increase, you need only exercise your option."

Tax Consequences

In the year when the executive receives his free shares, he must include their full value in his ordinary income. He is taxed at personal service income rates. In the year when he exercises his stock option, the option spread is also taxed as personal service income.

The company is allowed to deduct amounts equal to those included by the executive in his income, and in the same year.

Accounting Consequences

What we have here are two plans lashed together. In handling the accounting, we simply separate them and handle each plan according to the applicable rules.

Let's start with the free shares. The company must charge its pretax earnings with the product of the number of shares actually earned times the value of each at the end of the five-year period. However, unlike the situation with classic performance shares, the charge to pretax earnings is "capped." The company can't control the share price itself, but it can control the charge to earnings by decreasing the number of shares payable as the share price rises. Hence the company knows in advance that its maximum charge to earnings over the five-year period will be $50,000 and that the charge will be incurred only if earnings per share growth averages 10 percent or more per year. As a result, the charge is not only predictable and controllable but directly related to the underlying profitability of the company itself.

Since the nonqualified stock option is not discounted, no charge to earnings need be taken. Some dilution does occur, however.

The net result is that if the market price does not appreciate, the charge to earnings is the same for modified performance shares as for classic performance shares; and if the market price does appreciate, the charge to earnings is less than it would have been with classic performance shares.

Evaluation

From a strictly economic point of view, modified performance shares confer on the executive the same economic benefits as classic performance shares, except under a couple of conditions.

Suppose, for example, the company's earnings per share growth is so poor that the executive receives no free shares, but the market price of the stock rises anyway (an unlikely event). With classic performance shares the executive would not benefit from the market price increase, because he would receive nothing whatsoever. With modified performance shares, however, the executive would lose his free shares but would be able to exercise his stock option and benefit from the market price appreciation.

Or suppose the company's earnings per share growth is so poor that the executive receives no free shares, and the market price has reflected this poor performance by not moving at all during the five years or by moving downward. Once again, the executive would receive nothing with classic performance shares and would apparently receive nothing with modified performance shares either. But remember that he has two years left during which to exercise his stock option. Although the option is worthless now, it may yet take on value during the next two years. What's the point in moving to modified performance shares—especially when the resulting plan is so complex compared to classic performance shares? Well, the company gains from an accounting standpoint, but it has to give too. It has to give the executive an option with no performance strings attached.

Some companies have sought to gain the accounting advantages of modified performance shares without giving the executives any extra advantage. For example, one company tried to attach strings to the exercise of the nonqualified stock option. It told each executive he could exercise all his option shares only if the average growth in earnings per share during the five-year period was 10 percent or more. If growth was less, the executive stood to forfeit his opportunity to exercise some or all of the option shares.

But the company ran afoul of the accounting rules. Obviously, both the number of option shares and the purchase price per share were not known on the date of option grant; only the purchase price was known. The measurement date was therefore delayed from the date of option grant until the end of the five-year period. And because of this, any appreciation in the option had to be charged to earnings. This company ended up with all the accounting problems of classic performance shares and an excessively complex plan to boot.

Another company was troubled by the fact that the executive had a free ride on his option shares for two years beyond the performance period. That company decided to restrict the exercise "window" from two years to 30 days. This presented no problem for most executives in the plan, since they could buy and sell their option shares at will. But it limited the ability of the officers to sell shares at a profit without having to return the profit to the company.

In fact, many companies using modified performance shares have gone the other way. Since most companies granting nonqualified stock options extend the life of the option for ten years, and since there is no direct charge to earnings, they have allowed their executives a full ten-year exercise period—or, in our example, five years after the performance period.

Modified Performance Shares—Another Variant

Again, an incentive is offered: "You are hereby granted 500 nonqualified stock option shares at $100 each, the current market value of our stock. The options may not be exercised for five years, and then they are exercisable for two years, after which they will expire. You are also hereby granted the opportunity to earn $50,000 in cash or an

equivalent number of free shares. To do so, however, you must remain with the company during the five-year period. In addition, average growth in earnings per share during the period must equal or
exceed 10 percent per year. If it is less, the amount of cash or equivalent free shares you may earn will be decreased."

This simpler plan duplicates the basic modified performance
share plan in every respect save one. If the growth in earnings per
share is good but the stock price declines, the executive receives the
same payout as if the stock price had not declined.

To illustrate, assume that the earnings per share goal is met but
that the stock price declines from $100 to $50 per share. With basic
modified performance shares the executive would receive 500 shares
free, each of them worth $50. As an alternative he might receive
$25,000 in cash. With this next variation, however, the executive re-
ceives $50,000 in cash or, if the company wishes to pay him in shares,
1,000 shares. Thus he has been insulated from the market price decline, although he reaps the benefit of a market price increase
through his stock option.

In one sense, this kind of plan is troubling, but in another sense it
isn't. At first glance the executive seems to be receiving a reward no
matter whether the market price increases or decreases.

Viewed from another perspective, however, the reward stems,
not from the market price decline per se, but from the achievement of
a rigorous earnings per share growth goal. In that sense, the executive is not so much being rewarded for a decrease in the market price
of the stock as merely not being penalized for the decrease. After all,
if a stock option goes underwater, the optionee does not have his
bonus cut. He simply receives nothing from the option. That is essentially what is occurring here.

The tax consequences are the same for this variant as for basic
modified performance shares. However, the accounting consequences would be somewhat different if the market price should decline by the end of the period. With basic modified performance
shares the company's charges to earnings are less because of the market price decline. But such is not the case with this variant. Nevertheless, charges to earnings are predictable, controllable, and in direct
relation to underlying profitability.

Modified Performance Shares—Yet Another Variant

Yet again, an incentive is offered: "You are hereby granted 350 nonqualified stock option shares at $100 each, the current market value of our stock. The options may not be exercised for five years, and then they are exercisable for two years, after which they will expire. You are also hereby granted the opportunity to earn $70,000 in cash or an equivalent number of free shares. To do so, however, you must remain with the company during the five-year period. In addition, the average growth in earnings per share during the period must equal or exceed 10 percent per year. If it is less, the amount of cash or equivalent free shares you may earn will be decreased."

Companies adopting this variant are going to pour a lot more market price incentive down the drain and then top up the quart jar with a commensurately greater amount of incentive for internal results. At the same time, the executive receives more help in financing his option. Assuming the growth goal is met, he may receive enough cash to pay his taxes on the cash bonus and have enough left to exercise his option. Of course, he has to come up with the taxes on the option spread, but a company can go only so far!

Obviously, the company that opts for this approach has to be willing to take on more charges to its earnings statement. However, the charges are predictable, controllable, and, if the number of eligibles and size of awards to each are reasonable, in relation to the company's underlying profitability.

Book Value Plans—Actual Purchases

A very few publicly owned companies have sought to emulate the practices of privately held companies and have allowed their executives to buy shares outright at the then current book value per share. At some later date the executive is permitted to sell the shares back to the company, once again at the then current book value. In the meantime he receives the same dividends and voting rights as any other shareholder.

By itself, this plan insulates the executive from the market price of his company's stock, although it may be combined with stock options to obtain a desired blending of market price and internal performance incentives. It is a simple plan compared to some. It gives the executive long-term capital gains tax treatment when he sells his shares. It does not require any charges to the company's earnings, since it is considered a true capital transaction. But it contains a number of problems as well.

First, if the book value of a company's shares is substantially lower than the market value, the shareholders may scream. After all why should an executive get the same dividends and voting rights at a fraction of the price? On the other hand, if the book value of a company's shares is substantially greater than the market value, as has happened in a number of cases in recent years, the executives are likely to scream. After all, why should an executive get the same dividends and voting rights and yet pay more?

Second, the executive may be put into a cash flow bind. He probably has to borrow the funds necessary to purchase the shares. If his dividends are sufficient to cover his borrowing costs, that's fine. But what if there is no dividend or if the dividend is low in relation to his borrowing costs?

Third, the plan is not cost-effective for the company because the price the company pays to give the executive long-term capital gains treatment is the loss of its own tax deduction.

For these reasons, book value plans are frequently talked about but rarely implemented.

Book Value Plans—Phantom Grants

To overcome the disadvantages associated with actual purchases of book value stock, another very few companies have made phantom book value grants. In effect the executive is given a number of units, each equal to the book value of one share. At some later date the executive receives a check for any appreciation in book value. During the interval he also receives the dividends payable on an equivalent number of actual shares.

This plan solves the executive's financing problems and is cost-effective, since payments are taxable at personal service income rates and are deductible to the company. Charges to earnings must be taken. But in contrast to phantom stock grants, which are predicated on the actual market price of the shares, such charges are predictable and controllable.

But there are problems nonetheless. First, in a normal situation the increase in book value in any one year is equal to the company's earnings per share minus the dividends per share, if any. Since the executive receives the dividends as they are declared as well as the appreciation in book value, he is simply receiving an economic benefit equal to the earnings per share. That being the case, it would be simpler to avoid the book value concept and just give the executive a straight payment equal to the earnings per share.

But would a company really want to do that? In all the other plans we have been considering, the executive is paid off only if *growth* in earnings per share occurs—and rather vigorous growth at that. But in this plan he would be paid off under any and all conditions as long as earnings per share do not decline to zero. Thus this sort of plan could be construed as a giveaway.

On the other hand, suppose the situation isn't normal. Suppose the company buys in some of its shares. Or sells some new shares to the public. Or uses new shares to make an acquisition. In any of these instances, as well as in others, a change in book value could occur that would have little to do with executive performance.

For these reasons the phantom book value concept, like the actual book value concept, is frequently discussed but rarely implemented.

Dividend Equivalents

Another rarity in the world of executive compensation is the straight dividend equivalent. One company that uses this plan grants senior executives a number of units each year. Each unit entitles the executive to an annual payment equal to the cash dividends declared that year on a share of company stock. The units do not expire until the executive reaches age 85 or dies, whichever event occurs *later*. (Apparently, it is a matter of indifference whether the executive lives or dies!)

Dividend equivalents have one thing going for them: They are relatively inconspicuous. One unit doesn't amount to much, but put many of them together and you have a mighty river of compensation.

However, dividend equivalents are perverse. They offer executives the incentive to maintain and if possible increase dividends. That sounds fine to the average shareholder, but what sense would it make if increasing the dividend put the company in the position of having to borrow money from the bank to finance the business? Thus dividend equivalents can provide an unbalanced incentive and subject executives to a conflict of interest.

Restricted Stock

Restricted stock does not itself constitute a compensation device. It is simply a medium, much like cash, for paying an executive.

With restricted stock the executive is given a number of shares for which he may or may not pay anything. He cannot sell any of the shares until certain conditions are met. If he doesn't meet the conditions the shares are forfeited back to the company, the executive receiving nothing if he paid nothing, or receiving his actual purchase price if he was required to pay for the shares. During the period prior to the lapse of the restrictions, the executive is entitled to receive dividends on the shares.

As to tax treatment, within 30 days of receiving the shares the executive can decide to take into his ordinary income an amount equal to the aggregate value of the shares on the date of grant less any price he paid for them. Such income is taxed at personal service income rates. Further appreciation in the shares becomes a long-term or short-term capital gain, depending on how long the shares are held. However, if the executive does elect this tax treatment and then later forfeits the shares, he receives none of his tax payments back. For this reason, few executives would make such an election. Instead, the executive would pay no tax on the shares until the restrictions lapsed. At that point he would take into his ordinary income an amount equal to the value of the shares as of the date the restrictions lapsed less any amount he paid for them. Such income would be taxed at personal service income rates. Any dividends received during the restriction period would also likely be taxed at personal service income rates. (In effect, IRS doesn't see restricted shares as real shares until the restrictions have elapsed. Hence the dividends are treated as compensation for services rendered.) For its part, the company gets to deduct any income included by the executive on his tax return, and in the same year or years.

Earlier we discussed a classic performance share plan that promised the executive 500 free shares after five years, provided that earnings per share growth averaged 10 percent or more per year. If the company wished to use restricted stock with such a plan, the executive would be given 500 free shares right away and then would be told: "You may keep these 500 free shares and receive dividends on them during the next five years unless you voluntarily resign or are discharged for cause, in which case you will have to return the shares to the company for no consideration.

"Whether you keep the shares beyond the five-year period depends on our earnings per share growth during the period. If this growth is 10 percent or more per year, you may keep all 500 shares, and at that point, you are free to do with them what you wish. However, if earnings per share growth averages less than 10 percent per year you will be required to return some of your shares without consideration. For example, if this growth averages 9 percent you will be required to return 100 shares to the company." And so on.

Why would a company want to offer a restricted stock plan? Presumably to capitalize on the so-called territorial imperative principle, which postulates that a man will fight harder to keep property he already has than to obtain someone else's property. Under the original classic performance share design the executive comes home to his wife and says: "The company just promised me 500 free shares five years from now, if I meet certain conditions." His wife replies: "Big deal! The company is always making promises but we never get anything. Look what happened with those stock options."

With this alternative, however, the executive comes home to his wife and says: "Just feast your eyes on this beautiful stock certificate. The company just gave me these 500 shares for nothing, and they're ours forever—unless something goes wrong in the next five years." Every night before he goes to bed, the executive can happily admire his new treasure. Perhaps the prospect of having to give up what he already has will make him redouble his efforts to see that nothing goes wrong.

Thus restricted stock can be quite a motivational medium if the conditions under which the shares are to be earned are achievable. But if the company gets piggish and demands, not 10 percent growth in earnings per share, but 25 percent growth, the net result is likely to be negative motivation of the highest order.

Restricted stock can be something of an accounting problem for the company, since the share base increases the minute the shares are issued, while the consideration for the shares—that is, the charges to earnings—may develop over five years or even more. Thus earnings per share may initially feel more impact with restricted shares than with shares paid later. Moreover, restricted shares can present the same open-ended accounting liability problem as regular shares.

Best-of-Both-Worlds Plans

The great bulk of companies can be classified into one of three categories:

  ● Those that believe that the market price of their stock is the best—and should be the only—measuring rod of executive performance. If surveys show that most companies with similar beliefs grant their executives one quart of market price incentive, they do the same.

- Those that believe that the market price of their stock is not the *only* indicator of executive performance. They also believe executives should be rewarded and penalized according to long-term financial performance, such as growth in earnings per share. If surveys show that the 100 percent market-price companies grant their executives one quart of market price incentive, they grant their executives one pint of market price incentive and one pint of incentive for growth in earnings per share.
- Those that believe that the market price of their stock is not only *not* the best measure of long-term executive performance, but indeed is a poor one. They believe that executives should be rewarded and penalized solely according to long-term financial performance. Thus, they grant their executives one quart of incentive for growth in earnings per share.

There are also a few companies, fortunately very few, in a fourth category. These companies believe implicitly in giving their executives the best of both worlds.

One company in this last category does not give its executives one quart of market price incentive and zero incentive for growth in earnings per share; it does not give them one pint of market price incentive and one pint of incentive for growth in earnings per share; it does not give them zero incentive for market price and one quart of incentive for growth in earnings per share. Rather, executives are asked to choose between one quart of market price incentive *and* one quart of incentive for growth in earnings per share. To make sure the executive doesn't unwittingly make the wrong decision, the company graciously permits him to delay his choice for up to ten years so that he can see how much liquid actually flowed into each bottle.

A plan like this can be faulted on a number of counts. First, it is obviously a lusher plan than any of the company's competitors would offer. That alone is not so bad, provided the company has reduced or eliminated some other element in its total executive compensation package to assure that the competitive scales are not broken. But has it?

Second, the plan has the potential for generating more charges to earnings than the plans in either of the first two categories. What is more, these charges to earnings will occur at an unfortunate time, namely when the market price of the company's stock is down.

The third and most crucial problem with this plan involves ethics. Is it ethical to give the executive a fully competitive reward if the market price rises, but to offer him the same reward even if the market price doesn't rise, or indeed drops? Is it ethical to give the executive a fully competitive reward if growth in earnings per share is excellent over a period of years, but to offer him the same reward in the event that growth in earnings per share is poor, or even negative?

Consider a particular company's plan. This company starts out by giving an executive a 1,000 share undiscounted stock option at an option price of $100 per share. This 1,000 share option is equivalent in size to the grant that companies that utilize only options would make to the same level of executive.

The company also gives the executive a grant of 1,000 performance units. Reasoning that a 15 percent growth in earnings per share for five years coupled with a constant price/earnings multiple would cause a doubling in its stock (from $100 to $200) and hence a $100 appreciation in each option share, the company stipulates that five years later each performance unit will be worth $100, provided growth in earnings per share averages 15 percent per year during the same period.

At the end of the period, the executive can choose either to exercise his 1,000 share stock option and forfeit his 1,000 performance units, or to be paid the value of his 1,000 performance units and forfeit his 1,000 share stock option.

Implicitly what this company is doing is establishing a second, internally run market for its stock. The first market is the New York Stock Exchange, where the stock is buffeted by all sorts of pressures outside the company's control. If its earnings per share increase 15 percent per year, its stock may not necessarily double in five years. In some cases it might triple, but in other (more contemporary) cases it might drop to half.

The second market is represented by the performance units. Here, the company sets up a clean room where no contaminants are allowed. In this clean room, or perfect world, stock values always mirror growth in earnings per share.

The fortunate executives at this company are permitted a rare luxury: They can choose whichever stock market they like. If the external winds are favorable and the value of their company's stock on the New York Stock Exchange soars, they can ride with the New

York Stock Exchange by exercising their stock options. But if the winds are unfavorable, they can always duck for cover in the cozy stock exchange that the company operates out of its own headquarters.

Most investors have learned—sometimes the hard way—that rewards mirror risks. They can buy a high-grade corporate bond and get a good yield, but probably attain little in the way of appreciation. Or they can buy a convertible bond and get a smaller yield, but this is offset by the possibility of appreciation, provided the common stock into which the bond is convertible rises significantly above its current level. Or they can buy common stock and receive little or perhaps no yield, but have the possibility of very substantial appreciation. However, there is no investment vehicle around that offers both high yield and high appreciation.

At least there is no such investment vehicle around that is available to *those* investors. There *is* one available to the executives who have the good fortune to be working for the company we have been discussing. The Italian immigrant who observed that "there's no such thing as a free lunch" obviously never heard of that company.

Major Design Issues

If a company decides to move away from total reliance on the market price of its stock as the measuring rod of long-term executive achievements, it will have to confront and resolve a number of design issues.

Eligibility

If there are relatively few individuals in a company who have a substantial impact on current profits, there are far fewer who have a substantial impact on profits over the longer term. Many people may study the desirability of building a giant petrochemical complex, but few are around the table when the final decision is made.

This line of reasoning, which points to a small eligible group for a long-term incentive compensation plan, is borne out in examining the practices of the companies that have such plans. Many companies in the multibillion-dollar sales range with as many as 100,000 employees include only 25 to 50 executives in the long-term incentive compensation plan.

Buttressing this lean eligibility pattern is the fact that most such plans require charges to the earnings statement. Thus the company is faced with the choice of giving large awards to a few executives or small awards to many executives. When it comes to a difficult choice like this, senior executives are comforted to learn that there is a sound theoretical reason for giving large awards to a few executives.

But what is the company to do about the several hundred managers who may have been participating in an earlier stock option plan? The company is paying them competitive salaries and annual bonuses, but it also knows that other companies with stock option plans are continuing to give grants to managers at these levels.

One solution—and it is the most motivational one—would be for the company to soup up its annual bonus opportunities so that the combination of the base salaries and annual bonus opportunities for this group would roughly equal the combination of other companies' base salaries, annual bonus opportunities, and option grants. By definition, these managers do have substantial influence on current profits, and if they are to be paid competitively it seems reasonable to increase their annual bonus opportunities.

However, this argument founders on two pragmatic points. If these managers are to receive higher annual bonus opportunities, their bonuses may exceed those in the bottom rungs of eligibility for the long-term incentive compensation plan. Theoretically, this is not a problem, since under risk-reward theory, it is not unreasonable to demand that an individual give up something (in this case, a lowered annual bonus opportunity compared to those in lesser positions) to get something even bigger (in this case, eligibility for grants under the long-term incentive plan). But whereas senior executives have no trouble in grasping the concept that long-term incentives should be large and restricted to a few, they seem to have great trouble in understanding why a subordinate should ever receive more of anything than they do.

The second problem concerns charges to earnings. If the company restricts the long-term eligible group so as to keep down charges to earnings, and if it then increases annual bonuses for others as a quid pro quo for cessation of future option grants, it will obviously have to take the very charge to earnings it wished to avoid.

Although the motivational reasoning is poor, what most companies do is continue giving option grants (but not other long-term incentives) to the managers who had always received options but who will be ineligible under the new long-term incentive plan. These managers are younger, statistically speaking, and therefore have more needs for current cash. They also have the smallest borrowing capacity and are hence in the worst position to finance a stock option. Moreover, if the chairman of the board has little or no influence over the price/earnings multiple of the company's stock, how much influence can a middle manager have? The only thing going for this very pragmatic solution is that there are no additional charges to the earnings statement.

Length of Performance Period

In our earlier examples we discussed a performance period of five years. But is that always the right period for any company wishing to adopt a long-term incentive plan? The answer is no.

The length of the performance period should mirror the span between the time when a major decision is made and the time when the decision comes to fruition. That time span varies from industry to industry. In the food industry, for example, it takes about three years to build a major plant and about the same time to develop, take through test markets, and introduce a new product. So a performance period of about three years would make sense for companies in this category.

On the other hand, in the pharmaceutical, oil, and chemical industries the time span is a lot longer. It may not take that long to build a pharmaceutical plant, but it may take years and years to develop a new drug and win the government's approval. In the oil industry little time may be spent on developing new products, but it takes five years or more to build a refinery. In chemicals and petrochemicals it takes years to develop new products and years to build plants. Theoretically speaking, one could argue for a performance period of ten years or so, but practically speaking not many executives will wait around that long for a payoff. The longest period now being used is six years—by an oil company, appropriately enough.

Most other companies use periods of four or five years. And no company uses less than three years, because to do so would be to create a sort of second annual incentive plan.

Frequency of Grant

Suppose a company has decided to adopt a five-year performance period, and its first grant covers the years 1978 through 1982. When should the next performance period start? Not until 1983, after the first one has ended? At the beginning of 1979? Or at the beginning of some intermediate year?

What we are concerned with here is the degree of performance period overlap. And there are advantages and disadvantages to any approach.

The discrete approach. With the discrete approach, where there is no overlap between periods, the plan design is less confusing because each year contributes to only one performance period. Consequently, this approach may be viewed as more motivationally pure. But there are problems galore. First, other things being equal, the company will have to grant five times more award opportunity per performance period than it would if it were using overlapping annual grants.

What if the performance targets selected for the plan turn out to be too easy? Or too tough? What if an executive who was given a normal grant and who was thought to have considerable potential actually demonstrates no potential and in fact suffers a performance decline? Short of firing him, how is the company to get its money back?

Since there is five times the money riding on the discrete approach compared to the annual overlapping approach, won't executives be tempted to bring revenues from the sixth year into the fifth year and to defer costs from the fifth year into the sixth year, thereby reaping a huge payout? If the next performance period suffers because of this behavior, the executives can always quit.

What about an individual who joins the company or becomes eligible for the long-term plan in the middle of a performance period? Surely it won't do to make him wait several years until the trolley car comes around the bend again. But to include him in some pro-rata fashion may give him a windfall.

Finally, how about proxy visibility? If the chairman receives a base salary and annual bonus for the first four years and then a base salary, annual bonus, and huge long-term incentive payout in the fifth year, the various corporate audiences—shareholders, employees, unions—may kick up a storm.

The annual overlapping approach. Whatever the theoretical appeal of the discrete approach, it is a practical nightmare, whereas the annual overlapping approach is less theoretically appealing but makes a lot of practical sense. Most companies would make a contingent grant at the beginning of 1978 to cover performance during the period 1978 through 1982, another contingent grant at the beginning of 1979 to cover performance during the period 1979 through 1983, another contingent grant at the beginning of 1980 to cover performance during 1980 through 1984, and so on.

The biennial overlap. Some companies favor performance periods with biennial rather than annual overlaps. In this case, the first grant at the beginning of 1978 covers performance for 1978 through 1982, but the second grant is not made until 1980 and covers performance during 1980 through 1984. Awards are approximately twice as large as those under the annual overlap approach.

Proponents of the biennial approach point to the lessened administrative workload. But the company also risks more proxy visibility and will be more heavily affected if the performance targets prove too tough or too easy.

The retiring executive. Another issue that arises in connection with performance period lengths and frequencies concerns the treatment of executives who are close to retirement. If the company is using a five-year performance period and is making grants annually, what should it do in the case of an executive who will be retiring at the end of four years?

Should the last grant to this executive be made at the beginning of his last full five-year performance period? Or should the executive be given additional grants for the remaining four years and then receive some sort of pro-rata cash settlement when he retires? Or should he be given one grant at the beginning of the new period and then five years later (one year after retirement) receive four-fifths of the rewards because he served for four-fifths of the performance period? And should he be given still another grant for each of those remaining years on the job and then, when the performance periods end, receive his prorated share of each grant?

Most companies opt for the last alternative, and with good reason. If an executive is making decisions whose results won't be known for five years, he shouldn't be tempted to short-term it in the few years preceding his retirement. Instead, he should be held hostage to the consequences of his acts after his retirement. If he makes the right long-term decisions and leaves behind him solid successor management, he stands to reap extra rewards for several years after he retires. But if he doesn't, he should pay the penalty. Among other things, this approach also helps to ease the executive down into retirement income, instead of shoving him off a compensation cliff.

Performance Measures

Earlier we considered the pros and cons of various definitions of profitability. In the context of that discussion, the following points should be observed when designing long-term incentive compensation plans.

First, the onus is on the designer to defend his reasons for not predicating rewards on performance after taxes. Since the performance plan is wholly or partially in lieu of an option plan, and since the new plan is being designed to forge a direct linkage between performance which is in the shareholders' interests and the rewards the executive receives, it makes sense to define performance in shareholder terms. And that means performance after taxes.

Second, it probably also makes sense to define performance not only after taxes but after the costs of all incentive plans, including even the plan under consideration, have been charged against earnings. Otherwise, the following dialogue might ensue at an annual meeting.

> SHAREHOLDER: Mr. Chairman, I recall that five years ago the shareholders approved a new long-term incentive plan that offered full payouts if earnings per share grew an average of 10 percent per year during the next five years. I see from the new proxy statement that full payouts have now in fact been made. What I don't understand is how such payouts could have been made when earnings per share during the last five years grew only 7 percent per year.
>
> CHAIRMAN: I can understand your confusion, but the matter can be cleared up easily. You see, our earnings per share growth did average 10 percent per year during the last five years, but that was before we charged the costs of the payouts against earnings. Unfortunately, those charges dropped the earnings per share growth rate to 7 percent. But please remember we are following the plan you approved.

Question: Would the shareholders have approved the plan so readily if they had known how it really worked?

Most companies adopting long-term incentive compensation plans choose growth in earnings per share as the performance measure. However, there is a growing emphasis on using an ROI measure like return on shareholders' equity, return on capital employed, or return on assets. Sometimes the ROI measure is used alone, but more often it is combined with growth in earnings per share.

Of course, if long-term rewards are to be predicated on earnings per share growth, the question arises: Growth over what? Presumably, a company would select as its base period for growth measurement the earnings per share in the year immediately preceding the performance period. Certainly, that is the way most financial analysts would measure growth.

But what if the company is cyclical and the earnings per share in the base period year were unusually high or low? In that case, executives might have an impossible time achieving the objectives in the ensuing performance period. Or they might make the objectives in a walk.

For this reason, some companies prefer to define their base as the average earnings per share in the two or even three years preceding the performance period. This approach gives them a more stable platform from which to measure growth, but it may also give them too easy a time of it. Obviously, if earnings per share are growing over the long term the base earnings per share in most years will be lower than the earnings per share in the year immediately preceding the performance period. Companies meet this problem in varying ways. Some look at various possible base figures (single-year average, two-year average, three-year average) and then pick a figure they think makes sense. Others have developed mathematical approaches, and still others do nothing. They don't wish to be reminded that 10 percent earnings per share growth, when measured the way they measure it, is really only 8 percent growth the way everyone else measures it.

A last topic in this area concerns the question of divisionalization. Should the reward opportunities offered to the head of a major profit center be predicated on overall corporate earnings per share growth or on the cumulative profits of the profit center during the period? Theoretically, it seems clear that the latter pattern should prevail, provided that the profit center is truly autonomous, not exchanging people, products, or technology to any great degree with any other profit center. But in practice there is another issue concerning the company's ability to set valid, equal-stretch, long-term performance targets for each profit center. As we have seen, many companies have trouble in setting equal-stretch budgets for a single year. That being the case, only the rare company will have such solid long-range planning as to enable it to set equal-stretch targets over the longer term. Nevertheless, the possibility should not be dismissed out of hand.

Size of Awards

If a company that already has competitive base salaries, competitive annual bonus opportunities, and competitive stock option grants should want to add a new long-term incentive plan, something would have to give. What usually gives is the stock option plan. As implied earlier, companies cut down on the size of their option grants to make competitive room for the new long-term incentive plan.

In doing so, the company has to devise some rationale for determining the tradeoffs involved. For example, the company might have determined with respect to a particular executive that a competitive annual stock option grant made by companies granting only stock options would be for 1,000 shares at $100 per share. The company might wish to move from the use of options alone to a combination nonqualified option/cash plan. In effect, the company intends to couple the grant of each stock option share with the opportunity to earn $100 in cash provided that the growth in earnings per share averages 10 percent per year during the next five years.

Given these facts, the company might reason as follows. If an executive had a 1,000 share stock option at $100 per share, and if earnings per share increased steadily at 10 percent per year, and if the stock traded at a constant price/earnings multiple, and if the executive exercised his option at the end of five years, the stock would have appreciated from $100 to $161 per share. The executive would pay $100,000 for shares worth $161,000 at the time he purchased them. Therefore, his pretax economic benefit would be $61,000.

As an alternative we could grant the executive 379 option shares at an option price of $100 per share and then give him the opportunity to earn $37,900 in cash provided that growth in earnings per share averages 10 percent per year during the next five years. If that growth materializes, the executive receives $37,900 in cash. At the same time, if the price/earnings multiple remains constant, the market price of our stock will rise from $100 to $161. By exercising his 379 option shares at that time, the executive will receive a pretax economic benefit of $23,119 (379 shares times $61 spread). Adding this benefit to his $37,900 cash payment gives him a total benefit of $61,019—or the same as he would have received from a competitive stock option grant.

If the company followed the same method but decided to predicate the payment of full rewards on a 15 percent average annual growth in earnings per share instead of a 10 percent growth, it would find that it would need to grant the executive, not 379 option shares plus the opportunity to earn $37,900 in cash, but 503 option shares and the opportunity to earn $50,300 in cash. The reason is that the higher earnings per share growth assumption makes a competitive option grant that much more valuable, assuming the stock is trading at a constant price/earnings multiple.

As an alternative to triangulating from stock options, the company could study the practices of other companies with conceptually similar long-term incentive compensation plans. However, it had better be armed with a computer, since different plans have different performance periods, different frequencies of grant, different base periods, and different performance targets.

In general, however, the size of award opportunities is a function of the performance being demanded. That makes sense, because if you want a lot of performance you have to be willing to pay for it.

As this is being written, the common earnings per share growth objective required for a full payout is approximately 10 to 12 percent per year. Hardly any company would demand less performance than this, but few demand more either. The minimum earnings per share growth figure—that is, the point below which no awards are payable—typically is 5 percent, but several companies demand growth of at least 6 or 7 percent.

Note that growth is almost always expressed in cumulative terms. For example, suppose that the earnings per share before the start of the performance period are $1. Suppose further that the company is demanding 10 percent growth for a full payout. Compounding the $1 base period by 10 percent produces an implied $1.10 in the first year of the performance period, $1.21 in the second year, $1.33 in the third year, $1.46 in the fourth year, and $1.61 in the fifth year.

What the company is *not* doing is to offer the executive a full payout if earnings per share equal or exceed $1.61 in the fifth year. To do so would be to offer an annual incentive five years out, and he could forget about the intervening years.

What the company *is* doing is to offer the executive a full payout if earnings per share equal or exceed $6.71 during all five years taken together. This figure of $6.71 is the sum of the implied earnings per share figures in each of the five years of the performance period (excluding the base period figure). In effect, the company is indifferent to the incidence of earnings per share during the performance period. If earnings per share grow by exactly 10 percent each year, fine. But it is also acceptable, though unlikely, to earn $6.71 in the first year of the period, followed by four years of zero earnings per share. This indifference to the incidence of earnings per share growth is what makes the incentive plan truly long term. (Obviously, the company is not indifferent when it comes to making payoffs under the annual incentive plan.)

Forfeitures

As implied earlier, it is common practice to require a participating executive to forfeit any award opportunities which he has not yet earned if he voluntarily terminates his employment or is discharged for cause prior to the end of the performance period. Although this may seem like another application of the onerous golden handcuffs approach to executive compensation, the key words are *not yet earned.* A long-term plan is designed to pay off for performance over the long term. And a winner cannot be declared until all the votes are counted.

There is no tax requirement to impose this kind of forfeiture on the executive. But its use may help the company to hold talent, and executives don't seem to be troubled by it.

Perquisites_____8

Now we turn our attention to perquisites, an agglomeration of items designed to give the executive something extra.

There are three reasons why a company would want to give something extra—first, to confer status on the executive; second, to save him taxes; and third, to supplement broad-based employee benefit plans.

Status Aspects of Perquisites

We don't wear crowns in this country or carry such symbols of office as a field marshal's baton. So it's hard to tell the players apart, to spot the chairman of the board in a crowd. He's the one wearing the hand-tailored Savile Row suit, but you have to be knowledgeable about clothes to pick him out. You're more certain when you see him go by in a chauffeur-driven limousine. Or when you are ushered into his office, which is of such size that you think the New York Knicks must use it for practice in off-hours.

Status is a relative thing. Any tangible item, whether worth anything or not, that is given to certain individuals already perceived to be high in the hierarchy and that is withheld from other individuals perceived to be low in the hierarchy may take on status connotations. In many companies you can tell the players apart by the size of their offices. ("I have a three-window office. How many windows does your office have?") Or by whether they have a carpet on the floor.

In other companies the game is more subtle. Is there a water carafe on the desk? More important, does it have water in it? More important yet, does it have fresh water in it? What about the carpet? Is it a cheap nylon or is it made of wool? Sometimes the game is played with such vengeance that if the chairman of the board and the president dumped a load of trash in the center of their offices, the next day a dozen vice presidents would be clamoring for similar treatment.

All this is not to denigrate the exploitation of our desire for status. The intelligent exploitation of status needs can be less costly than increases in direct compensation.

Theoretically, status symbols are quite motivational. There is no question that many people work hard to get the corner office, to get the water carafe, and to get the company car. But once they get them, the company is usually loath to take them away for poor performance. Imagine the chairman of the board saying to an executive, "Jones, your performance last year was deplorable. Turn in your Rolls-Royce. This year, you'll be driving a Volkswagen Rabbit, and if I weren't so charitable you'd have to pay for your own gas." Jones's poor performance then could not be kept a secret; it would be visible in the parking lot every day. But few executives have the stomach for such strong action.

So executive perquisites may be quite motivational on the way to the top. But once the man is there, they are likely to have little further motivational value.

Tax Aspects of Perquisites

In the Coca-Cola Company it is rumored that only two people know the recipe for Coke, and they are destroyed every six months. That's how secret things are. But whenever anyone happens on some perquisite that carries a tax advantage, he trumpets the new-found knowledge at the next compensation conference he attends. Then other companies start doing the same thing and go around bragging about their coup. Sooner or later, when the IRS boys get wind of what is happening, regulations are issued to kill off that particular game.

At the moment hardly any perquisites give the executive a tax advantage. Take two, for example: company-provided automobiles and personal financial counseling. Suppose the company leases a car for an executive for $300 per month and picks up gas, oil, insurance, and other charges of $200 per month. During the year the executive drives 20,000 miles. Of this amount, 10,000 miles are for business and the remainder for personal purposes. (Travel to and from work cannot be considered a business expense.) If the executive is following the IRS rules, he will have to take into his ordinary income the sum of $3,000, representing half the $6,000 spent by the company on the car.

That being the case, what has the executive gained? Leaving aside the car's true business use, the executive received an economic benefit worth $3,000 and paid $1,500 taxes on it, leaving a net benefit of $1,500. If the company had instead given him an additional bonus of $3,000, he would have paid $1,500 tax on that too, and he would have had the same net $1,500 benefit. (Of course, the company might be able to use its purchasing power to lease the car at a cheaper rate than the executive could obtain on his own, and to that extent the executive does gain something extra and nontaxable.)

The same thing happens with personal financial counseling. Suppose the company foots the $3,000 bill for the executive to obtain a thorough analysis of his assets, income potential, and so on. Under IRS regulations he must include this in his ordinary income. He is then allowed to deduct from his income that portion of the $3,000 which represents tax advice. Assuming this is $2,000, the executive ends up paying a tax of $500 on the net economic benefit of $1,000. Alternatively, the company could give the executive an additional bonus of $3,000, and he could purchase his own personal financial counseling. He would then report $3,000 of additional income and take deductions of $2,000 against that income. Since he used the $3,000 to pay the personal financial counselor, he will have to come up with $500 out of his pocket—the same amount that would have been required had the company paid the bill for him. What has really been gained here, other than that the company has made sure the money was spent for personal financial counseling and not for betting on the horses?

This is not to imply that no perquisite has any tax advantage whatsoever. For example, it currently seems possible to give the executive a tax advantage by insuring him for all his medical expenses. But it does imply that the tax advantages of any perquisite are usually ephemeral. They may be here today and gone tomorrow.

Remember also that perquisites, all of them taken together, usually don't represent a big piece of the executive's compensation package. Perhaps assiduous analysis will reveal that a particular perquisite will save an executive $500 in taxes. But was the effort worthwhile, when the taxes on the executive's other income from the company will be $100,000? On top of this, the SEC now requires companies to include the value of all perquisites in the proxy statement, or to discuss their nature if a value cannot be assigned. So the game of using perquisites to hide true economic benefits is over.

Supplemental Benefits

Sometimes a company will find it necessary to give an executive something extra in the way of fringe benefits normally provided to all employees. Whether the company is conferring a true perquisite must be determined from the facts and circumstances of the particular case.

For example, suppose the company offers every employee company-paid life insurance equal to twice his salary but not more than $100,000. Obviously, an executive earning $100,000 ends up getting life insurance equal to his salary, or half the rate for other employees. Perhaps the company was required to take this action because the group insurance carrier refused to write more than $100,000 of group insurance on any single individual. Under such circumstances the company might decide to purchase an individual life insurance policy to provide the executive an additional $100,000 of coverage. Clearly, this does not reflect any intent to give the executive a perquisite. Rather, the company was giving him what it would have given him in any event, had it not been prevented from doing so by an outside agency.

The same thing has been happening of late in the pension area. With the passage of ERISA, the maximum pension payable from a qualified pension plan is $75,000, graduated upward by changes in the cost of living. Suppose the company's plan calls for a retirement benefit equal to 50 percent of final salary after a career of 25 years. If an executive's final salary is $200,000 after 25 years of service, his ERISA-limited pension will be less than the agreed-upon 50 percent. Once again, the company did not impose such a limit; rather, the limit was imposed from the outside. Accordingly, the company might want to adopt a supplemental pension arrangement. The executive would receive from the qualified pension plan whatever maximum benefit the plan could pay, but he would receive additional cash from the company to bring him to the 50 percent pension level.

Other supplemental benefit arrangements are less clear. Suppose the company decides to guarantee the executive, not simply 50 percent of his final salary after 25 years of service, but 50 percent of his final total cash compensation, including his bonus. Is such treatment consistent with the way other people are treated in the company? How are commissions for salespersons handled in determining pensions? If the treatment is consistent, it cannot be considered a true perquisite. Otherwise, there is room for some argument.

Nevertheless, various supplemental benefit arrangements for executives do go beyond the definition of equal treatment and accordingly can be considered to have some aspects of perquisites. For example, the company may adopt a pension supplement that guarantees a full 50 percent pension, not at age 65 and after 25 years of service, but at age 55 and after 15 years of service. This makes it easier to attract a 50-year-old executive from the outside, since that executive can still qualify for a good pension. And it simplifies the problem of weeding out a 55-year-old executive who has been with the company for 15 or more years and whose work is no longer up to par.

Companies should certainly consider all the possibilities before deciding on any perquisite. And they should certainly supplement broad-based fringe benefits as needed. But in the final analysis they should use considerable prudence. To have no perquisites at all may be a luxury the company can ill afford, given the modest cost associated with a relatively lean perquisite package. To grant executives every perquisite known may poison the atmosphere by creating too wide a gulf between the haves and the have-nots, may needlessly provoke the ire of the shareholders, and may motivate not executive performance but a searching IRS look at corporate and individual tax returns.

Epilogue _____ 9

Many topics have been discussed in this book, including the design of compensation structures, the use and abuse of executive bonus plans, the possibilities and pitfalls of deferred compensation, the problems inherent in stock option plans, and the need to offer executives viable incentives for long-term performance.

Throughout, one word has occurred with great frequency: *motivation.* This has been the subject of the book and should be the purpose of executive compensation.

Taxes are important to executive compensation. Technique is important. But motivation is *paramount.* To achieve it requires that

- Reward opportunities be meaningful and commensurate with the risks involved.
- Rewards vary with demonstrated performance so that the executive knows he can control his rewards by controlling his performance.

The concepts are simple; the execution is not. But the job is well worth trying, for the successful motivation of increased executive performance is always superbly rewarding.

Index

DATE DUE